Illustrated by Jessica Hobbs and
Belinda Austin

This book is dedicated to my beloved BRUTUS!

DIGITAL GIRL

0101010101010101010101

0101010101 0101010101

0101010101 0101010101

0101010101 0101010101

0101010101 0101010101

0101010101 0101010101

Cover designed by Belinda V. Garcia and Jessica Hobbs

This book is a work of fiction. Names, characters, places, and incidents either are products of the author's imagination or are used fictitiously. Any resemblance to actual persons, living or dead, events, or locales is entirely coincidental.

Printed in the United States of America
First Printing: October 2020
Science Misfits
ISBN– 9798552841448

DIGITAL GIRL, also, comes as a hilarious Audio Book

Digital Girl

Belinda Austin

B. Austin

Contents

PROLOGUE

S cience class was over. The teacher wanted to know why I did not turn in my homework.

"Computer-gnomes ate my homework," I explained. The science teacher looked clueless.

"Surely, a smart man like you, has heard of appliance-gnomes?" I said.

"I have no such knowledge of this new technology, Miss Jupiter," the balding man recited. He wore 1960 sandals, along with a blue sock and a yellow sock.

"Appliance-gnomes steal socks from clothes dryers."

He snapped his heels together and announced, "So that is what happens when the dryer stops spinning. Gnomes steal our socks! Thank you for enlightening me, Miss Jupiter."

I then explained that computer-gnomes are high-tech cousins of appliance gnomes. Computer-gnomes slap advertising across interesting online gossip, and commit other internet mischief.

"Well, well, so gnomes pop up those annoying ads," the science teacher said.

"Place your ear against the computer and you might hear tiny hammering or singing," I added.

He crawled beneath the desk, ripping his coffee-stained pants. He placed his ear against the computer tower case. "You are 100% correct! I can hear gnomes singing." The science teacher hummed along, sounding a lot like a tiny fan.

Suddenly, the camera on the monitor flashed, as if taking my picture. I didn't think anything of the malfunction at the time. I simply reached over and turned off the microphone of the computer. The light had been blinking.

I swaggered from the classroom.

Computer-gnomes ate my homework? I slid down the wall by my school locker, hugging my stomach and laughing. I am President of the Chaos Computing Club and would never, ever have any problems involving computers. I am a first-class computer hacker, my fingers flexed and always ready to type

300 words a minute. My mouse is vertical and roars like a gaming joystick. My keyboard can be shaped like an ergonomic tent, which allows me to camp out at my computer on weekends.

I picked myself up and headed home, proud of being the smartest person on the planet, or so I thought then.

The funny thing is though; lying about the past sometimes predicts the future. I learned the hard way that the tiny microphone in the computer, well, someone really is listening.

I bragged that I knew everything about computers, but I found out that sometimes, being too smart is a curse.

I discovered, the hard way, that the tiny camera on the computer, well, someone really is watching.

So, grab a soda and a slice of pizza. Get comfortable to hear a story that I swear, on all my hacking awards, is true! That creepy feeling you get, when you're by yourself, working on the computer at home, well, you really are not alone.

After everything that happened that night, I'm surprised to be alive to say this—be careful about tempting fate.

You see, it was a dark stormy night and...well, it turns out there really is such a thing as karma.

B. Austin, Belinda Austin

COMPUTER–GNOMES DO EXIST

Now here was the raw deal. My parents believed their two children would not spend so much time using the computer, IF the monitor had a screen that resembled a television set from the caveman era. My parents took away my cell phone, so I had to resort to this dinosaur of wires and glass to get online. Part of my nightly routine was to check if anymore of my Facebook friends had unfriended me. I was keeping a list labeled Meanie Tweenies. It's not easy being 12 years old and being called a dorky freak all over social media. It's not easy being a girl named Jupiter and being accused of being an alien.

As if the old monitor was a looking glass, my face stared back wistfully, revealing a freckled girl with mousy-brown hair hanging in strings to her shoulders. A storm earlier zapped the computer, breaking it, and ruining my evening plans of browsing the web and watching a ballet in Manhattan or Europe. Who cared if the performance was years old!

I yanked my ballet slippers from my neck, throwing them in the air with disgust.

Aha! The computer had a keyhole with an arrow pointing to the word *locked* engraved on the case. The machine must have turned to the *locked* position when lightning struck, turning itself off.

I ransacked the desk drawer for the computer key, but only found a lipstick tube, which I stuffed in my waistband. A girl never knew when she might run into a famous pop star, which is why I sometimes combed my hair. A megastar would require clean teeth and minty breath. I sprayed my fingers with Peppermint Monitor Cleaner and then rubbed my fingers across my teeth.

Ah, there was gold beneath the desktop, chewing gum that is. The gum tasted sort of like my spit. My brother Axel had a big mouth, like all boys, so this wad might be his.

I blew the bubblegum like a puffer fish.

The bubble popped at the same instance a thunderbolt exploded.

Sticky gum plastered against my computer eyeglasses that normally let me hack through the web like Superman with x-ray vision. Hackers talk to themselves since we spend loads of time by ourselves. "It's not my fault storms make me jumpy," I said.

"Not your fault?" echoed in the study.

Yipes! No one else was in the room.

"What's your login, eh, poodle?" the voice screeched.

The radio plug dangled from the desk, proving a radio announcer could not be talking.

Speakers hanging from the monitor could transmit a voice when the computer was on. However, the computer could not be working in the *locked* position.

The computer case was breathing! A ticking noise sounded like a beating heart.

The speakers squeaked, "Oh, dear, I'm going to be late."

"Caterpillar, is that you?" I whispered to my wise hacker friend.

There was a red picture frame on my bookcase shelf in the study. The frame held a picture of an avatar, an ugly, big-nosed, wormy caterpillar wearing large, black-framed glasses. An online user sometimes chose an avatar to represent him or her in the computer or internet. The hacker known as

Caterpillar was not only a friend but also my hero. Caterpillar was a legend among hackers. We occasionally took online vacations together. My avatar was a white rabbit.

"Login!" bounced off the study walls.

"You're freaking me out, Caterpillar," I screeched.

"I am talking to you, human. You have metal across your teeth and pimples on your nose. Log-in!"

I slammed a hand across my nose. "The spots on my face are freckles, you moron! Freckles!"

I yanked the computer's power cord from the wall.

There was no juice but still, "Skinny ninny!" hollered from the speakers.

"I am not skinny!" I shouted.

"Login! I need your name and password, you nincompoop!" the unplugged computer yelled.

Engraved in gold letters was the name *Enchanter* on a piece of shiny metal on the box that held the guts of the computer. Now, I, of all people knew that a computer was not magic. Enchanter was the model name of the computer, yet I said in a breathless voice, "Enchanter, is that you?"

A stick horse materialized on the monitor screen. The horse wore a French beret cocked jauntily on its skull. A mustache curled up on each side of its face. The horse rolled around the screen on a golden wheel. "I am risking my job by talking back to a mere user," the horse said in a snotty French accent.

The horse spun its head around its stick, as if to see if someone was spying. Quickly, it reshaped its head into a golden lock that resembled locks hanging from school lockers, except this lock had a flattened horse face.

7

The lock bounced, spitting as it spoke. "I am Monsieur Barebones, Head of Computer Security." Its keyhole moved like a mouth.

The lock slammed against the monitor, causing its horse face to fill the entire screen. "You, girly, I know who you are." The horse knocked against the glass with its face. "You are Jupiter, Offspring Version Two, who likes to blame others."

"But it *was* gnomes who broke the computer last week, just like I told Dad," I insisted.

"Eek! You have heard about the beasties!" The lock sprayed itself with a can labeled, *Gnome Repellent.* "The computer runs smoothly one moment, the next second, the machine is crashing. Gnomes are wafflers. The beasties help me plug a security hole, while spraying hoses at the firewall to let the pirates in. The raiders steal music, video, and other treasure. They sell their booty on the black market, PirateTreasureBay."

"Yeah, I know. My brother is a computer pirate, and you're lying. I made up computer-gnomes to claim they ate my homework!" I said.

"Shush, Jupiter, do not anger the gnomes. Instead, take teeny-tiny baseball hats, boots, and blue jeans. Stuff the clothes in the DVD drive, one at a time, mind you. Include ashes from your dad's pipe. A gnome loves used tobacco, as you do, Jupiter. I watched you pick up your dad's pipe and smell it. Ah, you can't get closer to your dad by sniffing his cold ashes."

"How do you know so much about me?" I said in a small voice.

"First thing your dad did when he set up this computer, was to load the hard drive with family files and pictures."

"Be quiet," I whispered because Axel was outside the door, rummaging with some tools. I had locked my brother out of the study and Axel was good at breaking into hardware, too. "Where are the family files?" I demanded. Maybe I could dig up some dirt on Axel and blackmail him in the future.

Barebones was about to answer but then a humming came from the computer—a mishmash of voices blended into noise. Behind Barebones was an animated background image. Padlocked iron gates guarded a dark and murky dungeon. Gawking eyes floated in the darkness. The eyes were bloody, and it appeared as if dozens of dragons lurked in the dungeon.

Ah, *Dungeons and Dragons*, my brother's favorite game. Axel must have changed the background.

Barebones neighed like a horse and beckoned with its wide nostrils. "Come closer, Jupiter."

I have always been a sucker for a handsome stick horse. The stud's mane stuck straight up from its horsey head with hair gel. Ooh, just my style.

I flattened my ear against the monitor.

Barebones whispered, "The beasties who infest this computer insist I unlock the gates and let them at you."

"Why?"

"They think you are a scheming, lying, freak," the horse said.

"Shut up! You are keeping me from surfing the Internet, so, scram, dog-food head!"

9

"There is no reason for insults, pimple face! Do not make me crosser than a French croissant. Your dad downloaded me for free from shareware, just to keep you out, Jupiter."

A familiar ache sank low in my stomach. *I am not a freak! I am not!*

"I read the documents your dad has on you in a file labeled, *Irresponsible Jupiter*," the horse sang. Barebones stuck its tongue out. Well, maybe not a tongue, more like a wire piece fashioned to pick a lock.

Barebones turned back into a stick horse cloaked in a trench coat and Sherlock Holmes hat. Its clothes had online-store sales tags. The horse peered through a magnifying glass, its eye covering the entire screen. "As Manager of Security, downloaded from the French Internet for free, I am programmed mainly with spyware. You show potential in your funny-looking photos. You are aged 12 years, like stinky cheese. Give yourself a chance, puppy; you may yet shine. Next time you throw your ballet shoes in the air, dance with them in the clouds. You are a soufflé, still rising. One day, you may be famous and a Quiche Jupiter named after you, voila!"

"I am already famous!" I swung my ballet shoes back around my neck, smacking the monitor with one shoe.

"No one has heard of you. Jupiter is a girl with but one Facebook friend," the horse said.

"Just one? Really? Geez, two friends unfriended me this week."

"Loser!" The horse stuck its tongue out and a bit of hay fell from its mouth. The horse was missing a front tooth.

I was about to reveal my secret hacking identity when the stick horse goaded me about the secret file again.

"I want to read that file! I'll guess the password." I pounded the chair-arms and hunched my back, spreading my fingers. I attacked the keyboard, slamming my fingers on the keys.

I turned the keyboard upside down, holding it in the air and typing.

I spun the keyboard back around, playing it like piano keys, from right to left, up and down.

Meanwhile, a screwdriver jiggled the door handle, followed by cursing. "I must hurry before Axel breaks in and kicks me out of the study," I muttered.

I closed my eyes, blindly clicking at the keys and laughing at my expertise. I clobbered the keys, stopping now and then to wipe my runny nose on my arm.

"Halt!" Barebones bounced across the monitor from corner to corner. "You...you cracker."

"Crackers are thieves, whereas I hack. Hackers are not malicious or destructive. We're just nosy and we tweet a lot of gossip."

"Hackers are trolls then," the horse said. "No wonder you have no friends."

I lifted my chin proudly. "I am not a troll. I do not fight with people online, and I always apologize if I upset anyone. On the web, I go by the handle White-Rabbit."

"Eek! The White-Rabbit!" Barebones sprayed itself with a can of *Cracker-Off*! "You are famous for breaking into the *Teen Choice Awards* and having your avatar hop across the television screen."

I laughed. "Yeah, the *Teen Choice Awards* was one of my better hacks. My avatar, White-Rabbit, looked so funny standing on the stage munching a carrot. Everyone believed the animation was part of the show until they read the words: **You have been hacked by White-Rabbit.** In the computer world, White-Rabbit represents me. The *Teen Choice Awards* was one of my prouder hacks."

"You have no real friends. You experience life on the internet, indirectly through your avatar!" Barebones aimed the *Cracker-Off* can and pushed the spray. This was turning out to be a weird Friday the 13th. *Cracker-Off* was packaged in such a strong cyber-aerosol can that the liquid shot right through the monitor screen, soaking my forehead.

The repellent did not even slow my fingers down on the keyboard.

"I insist you desist, and resist cracking the secret password," Barebones shouted.

A thunderous, lightning crack caused the monitor to flicker.

Even Mother Nature could not stop me.

"So electrocute me for hacking," I yelled.

"I just might do that," Axel yelled from behind the door. "Let me in, Jupiter!" He rattled the door handle but the door held.

A mighty thunderbolt shattered the study window. Glass flew everywhere. I covered my head, screaming.

Light flashes streaked across the screen.

"Duh, restart computer. Reboot. Restart computer. Reboot. Re...," Barebones stammered.

Whoosh!

Barebones vanished from the monitor screen.

The locked gates burst open. Computer gnomes ran out. The gnomes wore caps over their long hair and shoes that were too big for their feet. Some gnomes seemed to just be wearing grandfatherly beards. They were an inch or so in height, er, shortness.

The gnomes glared from beneath bushy brows.

The gnomes kept charging the monitor screen and flattening against the glass.

Axel pounded the door with his fists, yelling, "open up, Jupiter!"

I smirked at the monitor, giving the gnomes a smug, come-and-get-me look. Of course, the gnomes were animated GIFs. The gnomes were simply several, constantly-changing images to simulate movement. The gnomes could not really *get at me* as Barebones claimed the little buggers wanted to.

Why I could smash the gnomes like bugs. I brought my tennis shoe down hard on the floor just to show them my power. I giggled because the gnomes were digital and looked like characters in an animated film. I stuck my tongue out at the monitor, and the gnomes went crazy doing back flips and screaming.

This was kind of fun. The gnomes seemed to be interactive, which was weird for animated gifs. "The syncing of their moves with my actions, must be a coincidence," I mumbled.

A grunting noise came from the camera mounted on the left of the monitor.

The camera lens popped out, smacking my forehead.

One by one, gnomes jumped from the camera hole. With each camera flash, a gnome shot from the lens and into the study.

I swatted at the gnomes with printer paper. Darn but the tiny creatures were fast.

Gnomes climbed in my nose.

"Don't do dat," I said, sounding like a stuffy cold.

I sneezed. Gnomes flew out of my nostrils, smashing against the monitor.

Gnomes grabbed paperclips and snapped them open, stabbing my fingers.

Three gnomes carried a ballpoint pen and charged my stomach.

"Ouch!"

Other gnomes held up the stapler, firing staples like cannon balls.

Gnomes pinched my ankles, growling and biting.

Giggling Gnomes slid down my nose.

Other gnomes bounced on my eyelids.

"Stop it!" I yelled and swatted at a group of gnomes who were dragging a pair of scissors up my cheek, to cut off my eyelashes or stab me in the eye. The scissors clattered to the floor, breaking, thank goodness.

The cute little people really were beasts—a couple of gnomes were trying to saw off my hand with a letter opener. The tiny creatures were sneaky. While other gnomes attacked with office supplies, stronger gnomes tied my wrists and ankles with Velcro used to hold computer cables together. The gnomes took my picture for some creepy reason.

Gnomes climbed from my shoulders to my head, using my hair strands like ropes. The gnomes dug their dirty feet into my hair, making my scalp itchy.

"Get Off," I mumbled since several of the little buggers hung from my lip.

Gnomes chomped at my ears.

Gnomes stomped on my face and yanked my eyelids down.

One gnome, who seemed to be in charge since he was the only one wearing a red sash, stood on top of the camera with his fists on his hips. "Say, sorry," the gnome said with a lisp.

"Sorry for what?"

"Sorry for trolling us."

"I never did anything to you beasties!"

"You told the world's social media that computer-gnomes ate your homework."

"Axel, help," I shouted.

My brother was hammering the door hinges to remove them. Consequently, Axel could not hear anything but the banging against the door.

Another thing I learned about gnomes was that they have big mouths. However, gnomes were not very loud due to their being hoarse from always smoking.

The gnome standing on the camera said, "Oh our ears and whiskers, we are late for tea." He jumped on the button, flashing a red light in my eyes. Click!

At the same time, a lightning bolt crashed through the broken window, causing the camera flash to splash the room with light and electricity.

Electric sparks tingled from my head to toes. My teeth rattled fiercely, my upper teeth, switching places with my lower teeth.

My body was lifted into the air, spun, flipped, and then turned back around. I clenched the chair-arms and was still sitting, dangling in mid-air, with the seat far below. My head scraped the ceiling.

"Help me, Axel, please before something bad happens to me!" I let out a bloody scream.

A gnome smacked Velcro across my lips, silencing me.

An elderly gnome with a big, pointy nose yelled some magic words, pointing his fingers at me.

Whoosh! I shrunk to a tiny girl and floated down towards the desk.

Five gnomes held out a silky, grey scrap of material used to clean the monitor.

I bounced on the peppermint-smelling thing.

Before shrinking me, the gnomes had removed my shoestring. They now flung the shoestring over the monitor where the gnomes attached it with tape.

The gnomes pulled me up the shoestring to the camera mounted on the monitor. One by one, the gnomes jumped into the camera hole. The remaining gnomes tried to shove me down the hole. My tiny legs dangled in the camera hole and I clenched the edge.

The door busted open. Axel stood there breathing heavily. His shaggy brown hair was in his eyes. "There's a bug on the camera," he said.

"No, it's me, Axel!" My words were muffled because Velcro covered my mouth.

"Where's the fly swatter so I can kill it?" he growled.

Yipes! Axel really hated bugs.

A gnome poked my fingers with a thumbtack.

Yipes again.

I let go.

Yipes! Yipes! Yipes!

I vanished down the camera lens, swirling into a place filled with computer-gnomes.

I looked up.

Axel's big eye stared down the camera lens. "Hey, bug, you better not break the camera! You show your face again and I'm gonna smash you." Axel shook the camera.

The shaking caused me to snake down a tube and fall into the guts of the monitor.

Good, now Axel will see me on the screen.

I groaned at the sound of Axel walking out of the study.

B. Austin, Belinda Austin

I'M STRETCHED LIKE A LICORICE STICK

There was a loudspeaker announcement: "Attention all avatar shoppers! A pirate ship has just docked at memory Chip 342-2889-98881-05-5332-8788."

The gnomes snapped into smoke and vanished.

The noise of sparks, sizzling from wires dangling from the ceiling, caused me to nearly jump out of my skin. This place was dark and eerie. No horror film was ever this scary!

The storm must have caused electrical burns to smudge a glass wall. In the waistband of my tights was a tissue. I rubbed a spy hole into the fuzzy glass wall and placed my blurry eye against it.

The keyboard was below. There were no gnomes jumping on the keys.

I rubbed with the tissue until the entire glass wall was clear.

Directly in front was the mirrored closet in the study. The mirror reflected a small girl standing in a frame.

I flattened my nose against the glass wall, and the face grew bigger in the mirror across the room. The glass wall was like a magnifying glass.

I pulled at my hair and the image I thought frozen pulled at her hair. The rectangle that framed my face like a picture was the monitor frame. The gnomes trapped me inside the monitor! This was the worst day ever of my entire life!

For no reason, my user account kicked in. My animated GIF image hurled towards me.

Holy tornado! I created the GIF from my photo, but now the GIF and I resembled clones. We were both the same size except she was flat.

Funny thing is I never programmed my GIF with audio. She now sang, "I can't go back to yesterday because I was a different person then. Who in the world am I? Ah, that's the great puzzle."

Ugh! I charged forward, slamming against the monitor screen. Ouch! That hurt! My panicked face was reflected in the study mirror. My tear-filled eyes looked wild with fear.

A gust of wind howled through the study window, which the storm had shattered. I could see Axel carrying a roll of wide duct tape and a stepping stool, along with a window-sized piece of plastic.

I ripped the Velcro from my mouth. "Help," I screamed with all the power of my lungs. My voice was no louder than an ant.

My tiny hands pounding against the monitor screen could not make the noise of a dropped pin. I yelled and cursed until my voice was hoarse.

"I now realize that the gnome's magic changed me from a human girl to a digital girl, but the pain in my chest is of a real heart, woven with blood veins, not electrical wires. My memory banks are intact, and I am still Jupiter." My heart beat in my squashed chest. My mind still functioned in my flat head. My tiny stomach growled with hunger.

Real tears dripped down my cheeks. The tears tasted salty like a human girl.

My GIF image once more twirled by. My body was flattened and miniaturized but there was proof of my humankind. My animated image never changed its pattern, unlike me. I wiggled and jumped whenever I wanted and however my desire, because although I was now a digital girl, I was a human digital girl.

"Horrors, it is not logical for a person to be inside a computer monitor! How then is it logical to escape, or am I stuck inside the computer forever?"

Eek! My important computer glasses, which sometimes doubled as a hairband, had vanished. "Boogers! The gnomes stole my glasses!" That is the second pair to vanish this year, "but the last time wasn't my fault either."

Wow! Inside a monitor, there was no need for eyeglasses. The study was as clear as rainwater. The now armless desk chair rocked, its springs creaking.

One chair-arm was on the study floor. I was holding the other chair-arm when the gnome shrunk me. I hugged the tiny chair-arm to my chest, rubbing my cheek against the leather. "There's no place like home."

There was a roar like a tornado, causing my background theme to crash. A rainbow replaced the wallpaper on the monitor. Ruby-colored shoes fell at my feet. On closer examination, these were not ruby jewels but ruby computer circuits made in the shape of fashionable wedge heels.

"Yippy! The computer God sent a gift!" I kicked off my sneakers and shoved my feet into the ruby shoes. The shoes were a bit tight.

I clicked the shoes together and rainbow-colored electrical sparks flew from the soles, along with a zapping sound. "There's no place like home. There's no place like home," I sang, closing my eyes.

The tapping of my shoes formed another rainbow.

The shoes laughed while fizzling to smoking, emerald-colored embers.

The ashes spelled out the words: **You have been hacked by Oz!**

I peeped out from the screen to the study mirror.

Oh, my! The W-W-W hacked my computer. The W-W-W was head of the Oz hackers and went by the handle Wicked-Witch-West. The witch was actually a cracker, a thief, looking for gold at the end of the rainbow. She sent five Oz hackers to search the Internet for cracks. I was not fooled by the adorable little dog. That doggy avatar represented the smartest of these hackers working for the witch.

The hackers, Dorothy and her friends, were trying to figure out how to get over the Rainbow of Social Media Influencers. *Duh! Try walking under the rainbow, Scarecrow, but remember to tell the Tin-Man to duck his head. No wonder you all owe money to the Wicked-Witch-West and have to work as her slaves.*

The other avatars caught in the witch's web, were a flying monkey and a lion.

"I'll dig up your money someday, White-Rabbit," a voice cackled.

"I don't have a bank account, Witch," I yelled.

"I'll sell your human identity to the highest bidder, Jupiter." Her wicked laughter faded along with her face.

I was busted! The witch knew who the White-Rabbit really was now. Of course, I always hack using my avatar, White-Rabbit. I never should have bragged to Barebones, the security software, about being the White-Rabbit. The witch will tell my enemies the White-Rabbit's real identity. Thank goodness, she doesn't know that I'm a digital human girl. She must think I am an animated GIF like my screen saver. No telling what will happen, if she discovers my human form is actually stuck inside the hardware. "There must be a way out!" I thought with growing panic.

"I'm not sure what a monitor's guts are called, some sort of hardware, which is quite logical." I tapped my fingers against the rocklike monitor screen. "Oh, it's so hard to be stuck inside hardware." My head sounded hollow. "Hmm, I suppose, humans are a mix of hardware and software. My brain is soft, but my skull is hard. My thoughts must be software, which explains my squishy brain."

Button rows lined the monitor screen. This first button looked promising until the monitor darkened. When pushed again, the monitor flooded with light. Good. The button is a toggle button, which is why pushing the button toggled between darken and lighten.

Another button shifted me to the right so that half of my body was visible in the monitor. "Oops! My tiny stomach growled with hunger. Shift back to the center of the screen."

The next button lengthened me so that my head pushed against the monitor ceiling. "Too tall!" Stretching like a licorice stick, I reached out an arm and pushed a button which made me shrink back.

The next button caused me to stretch sideways.

"Too fat," I yelled, pushing the button and shrinking back to my preferred size.

"Perhaps this other button." I rode down like in an elevator, sinking lower and lower. "Hurry, push the button before you vanish!"

I rose back up until all of me was visible.

Three more buttons to go.

"Maybe, the *Monochrome* button is an escape button, whatever monochrome is." This button made all color fade from the screen. "Too pale!" Pushing the *Monochrome* button again, painted the screen with color.

"This button reads, *Refresh*." The monitor light flickered and a giant hand grabbed my neck. The hand slammed me against the screen and then yanked me back. The hand shook so hard that my teeth flipped back so the uppers were on top and the lower teeth on the bottom gums.

"Please stop," I bleated, crying like a goat.

The hand let go. Ouch! It then very gently placed a mirror on the floor before vanishing.

My hair was no longer puffed but combed in my favorite stringy fashion. "Refreshing!"

The last button read *Degauss*. An electric bolt shot at my wiggling body and lit me up with cobalt-blue lights. Magnets came out of the monitor wall. The magnetic force pulled at my fillings, yanking at my braces.

"Ouch! Quit pulling my teeth out!"

At last, the bolt of electricity fizzled to a few sparks. The magnets retracted back into the monitor walls.

My hand was no longer wiggling so I could stuff my fingers in my mouth without poking my eye out. Thank goodness, all the teeth were there and the two fillings. The trouble was my parents were going to be angry because my braces were scattered on the monitor floor in metal pieces.

Hopefully, the monitor adjustments gained Axel's attention.

My doofus brother just walked out of the study, yawning. It was past midnight. Darn Axel! Why did he not wonder where his sister was?

Now that Axel was gone, earth seemed like a distant planet. The worst part—the degaussing folded me into a freakish-looking staircase. My body waved about like an accordion playing a tearful tune.

Crying never helped anybody out of a frightening crisis, I thought. *Do not let fear get the best of you! Be brave else, you will never get out!* However, I was flat and now wrinkled like a folded piece of paper. My situation could not get any worse or so I thought!

The grinning head of a cat wearing a fishing hat bobbed in front of me, a cat fishing for the Wicked-Witch-West.

The witch's Familiar closed one eye, as if it was looking through a telescope, and examined me.

"Scram, tuna-breath," I said.

"Interesting, you are human," the cat hissed.

Slowly, the Familiar's head faded.

"Please come back. Don't tell the witch I'm human," I cried.

I left a note on the monitor screen, writing with lipstick: *To Whom It May Concern—help! Computer-gnomes kidnapped me!*

I added to the message. *It is not my fault! I did not break the study window.* I signed the message, *Jupiter* with a swirly *J*!

I had no choice but to walk even further away from the monitor screen and into the unknown. It was both scary and exciting to think that there might be a secret world beyond the dark murky dungeon of computer security, besides gnomes and hackers.

I MEET A MOUSE
NAMED LOUSE

The monitor acted like a magnifying glass when I was closer to the screen. The further away, the more I shrank into an itsy-bitsy, digital girl. The monitor ceiling was now high.

My accordion body bounced crookedly through electronic parts.

A sleeping, blue mouse hung by an extraordinarily long tail from a tree branch. His nose was shaped like a wheel. The tip of his tail was molded into an old-fashioned computer connector. Nailed to the tree was a sign with misspelled words that read, *Gided Computer tours by Louse-the-Mouse. Cheapest. Bestest Driving Tour this side of the Inturnet.*

I cleared my throat and said, "Please, Sir Louse, I need a guide to take me out of this place."

The mouse snored.

"Wake up, cheese breath!" I shouted, flicking his nose wheel.

Its nose spun furiously as the mouse swung around the tree branch, unwinding from his blue tail.

The mouse whizzed by too fast to grab him. It spun, until the mouse unwound from the tree. The mouse flew straight down. It flipped open its eye which flashed red like an ambulance light.

The mouse was big and landed with a thud, smashing against me.

The mouse landed on the black monitor floor with one ear folded back. Its purple tongue hung from its mouth. Its wire whiskers were bent out of shape. The mouse's breath smelled like lemon-scented furniture polish. Its tail stuck straight up in a question mark.

"Whatever is wrong with you, mousey, it's not my fault," I muttered.

"Program crash! Restart. Restart. One. Two...oh, Louse has a headache. Headache," the mouse said. The mouse sat up, holding its head in its paws.

A computer mouse often snacked. Cookie crumbs were stuck on Louse-the-Mouse with dried cola.

The mouse made a grinding noise like an engine and gave two clicks with its tongue. The mouse shook its rear end.

My head touched my lap, covering up my arms and hands, which prevented me from punching the mouse.

Louse sniffed in a circle. "Well? What are you?" the mouse said.

"I can't explain myself, I'm afraid, because I'm not myself, you see."

"Well, you're certainly not me, so you must be you," Louse said.

"You clobbered me," I said, sounding nasally. "Would you mind helping?"

The mouse grabbed me with its paws and wiggled me until my staircase-shape unfolded. I was still not my normal self but shaped like an accordion.

I pointed to the sign advertising tours. "You don't know how to spell."

"A mouse has no need for a spell checker. Is that what you are? A spell checker? Huh? Huh?" Louse moved one red eye closer. "You stink like sweat, sticky chocolate, bedpost gum, orange soda, and cheap roll-on deodorant. Aha, a thankless user!"

"I do not stink and get your yucky tongue off me!"

"You smell like user stink," the mouse said and rolled on its back, shivering. "I love users. Please, please touch Louse." The mouse pushed its belly out.

The mouse was ticklish and purred like a cat.

"You didn't use the mouse clicker to sneak in, did you?" Louse said.

"I never clicked the mouse but used the keyboard."

"Ah, a cracker," the mouse said.

"I am not a cracker. Gnomes kidnapped me."

"Did the gnomes tell you where they hid their pirate treasure?" Louse shoved its eye in my face. "Huh?"

"What treasure?" I said like a robot because Louse was an optical type mouse and hypnotizing. The mouse was cool looking with green and purple lights clashing on its sides.

"The documents gnomes steal, such as the memory they rob, missing years from the calendar, movies, music, photos, icons, diaries, bank receipts, and various sundries. All their booty is given to pirates," Louse said.

"The Wicked-Witch-West may be involved, either in my capture or my escape. Her hackers are in the area. So is her Familiar."

The mouse screamed, "The W-W-W's cat is around! We must hide!"

"First, something to eat," I said, rubbing my empty belly.

"Hang on and follow Louse." The mouse shook its tail in my face.

Louse tucked its chin into its chest and rolled like a ball. I skipped after him, holding onto its tail, which circled my arm. This was like skipping rope.

As computer mouses sometimes do, Louse got confused. It bounced in a corner, like a ball. "Oh dear, dear, Louse must find his center. Center," the mouse stuttered.

Louse rolled faster, in bigger circles.

Louse's tail entangled my legs, dragging me along.

"You're making me dizzy," I yelled.

"There. There," Louse said, patting its own head.

"Quit repeating yourself before I bop you!"

Louse smacked its cheek. "Louse has its center back and is stable. Oh, dear, Louse's tail is tangled."

The mouse rolled about, untangling its tail.

Once again, Louse tucked its chin into its chest and rolled like a ball.

I stumbled behind.

Suddenly, a large pencil eraser appeared and swiped at Louse.

"Help! I'm melting," the mouse screamed.

The eraser rubbed out the stomach, leaving a big hole.

I beat at the eraser with the chair-arm from the study.

The eraser wiped out a few of my hair strands, and I jumped out of the way, screaming.

The eraser bounced on Louse's wheel and rubbed.

The mouse's whiskers faded from view.

Then its face vanished, followed by its body.

Finally, its tail disappeared.

All that was left of Louse were mouse droppings and a few black arrows pointing to where it had been.

So, what if Louse was computer hardware? In this world of digital beings, the mouse was real. It had guts, even if the intestines were wires. The mouse had an intelligence of sorts, although it lacked memory. Louse had feelings and giggled when tickled. The mouse said it loved users.

"I won't cry, but oh, the same fate could still happen to me!" I sniffled and wiped my nose with my arm.

Without a mouse, I was lost in this strange computer world!

"Lions and tigers and bears! Oh, my!" echoed from the monitor.

That dreaded giggling had blasted from the computer speakers many times before.

"So, you need a mouse? Well, here I am!" a squeaky voice hollered.

My knees shook as an avatar slowly faded into view.

A white mouse, standing upright and wearing glasses on his mean face, glared at me. The mouse had big ears and wore a small straw hat. He wore a red bow tie and grey-and-white checkered shirt. Red suspenders held up his rolled-up denim pants that had hearts on them. Beneath the cuff of the pants were white-and-black-striped socks.

Louse-the-Mouse had been hacked and erased by this ten-year-old nightmare whose handle was Dormouse. The fifth-grader held a grudge for being kicked out of the Nerds Computing Club.

"Jupiter, you pile of rabbit poo," he screeched.

Dormouse was aware of my human identity!

31

His whiskers wiggled, a sign that Dormouse was about to explode from his anger. He pulled down his overalls, and waved his fanny.

If you have ever been mooned by a computer mouse, it was probably Dormouse hacking in. The ten-year-old pervert got his kicks by taking control of computer mouses and popping up unsavory websites on computers. Dormouse was giving our computer club a bad name, which is was why we kicked him out.

"You're not showing me anything I haven't seen before, creep," I yelled at his furry mouse fanny.

A DORMOUSE HIJACKS
ME

Dormouse cussed up a storm. He threw cheese. I caught a piece of cheddar. Thank goodness, since I was a digital girl the food was real to my virtual stomach. I gobbled the cheese. "Thanks. I was hungry."

"Ugh!" he screamed. "You want your tea and eat cheese, too! I'm going to drown you in a teapot!"

A teapot suddenly appeared.

I ran around in circles, avoiding the pouring spout.

Dormouse chased me, shouting, "There's no place like home!" He peeled the chair-arm from my fingers and threw it on the monitor floor.

He grabbed my hair and yanked.

"Ouch! That hurts, you jerk!"

"You are feeling pain without wearing virtual reality gear? Where in the stinky cheese is your White-Rabbit getup? I ain't ever seen you looking like a paper doll before." He slapped his knee, laughing. "You got yourself in some fix, bunny! It's true like the Familiar reported. You are a human digital girl!"

"You're working for the W-W-W now?" I said, feeling more scared by the millisecond.

"No one else would take me in after you squealed!" He kicked my shin. Dormouse growled at me hopping on one leg. "You cannot imagine what it is like being a dormouse working for a witch. She threatens each day to feed me to her cat. On top of that, the Familiar has it in for me ever since I poked the kitty's eye out."

"So that's why the Familiar keeps his eye closed."

Dormouse spit and snarled in a jealous manner. "So, what's it like being a human inside the computer instead of having to use an avatar to get around?"

"Scary. I fear that everyone wants a piece of me to make money. I may be the most valuable human who ever lived." I slam a hand across my big mouth but thank goodness, Dormouse had an attention disorder. The mouse switched topics.

"The witch knows my human identity. She threatens to tell my mother about my hacking. And it's your entire fault, Jupiter!" Dormouse kicked my other leg and I fell on his shoes.

"You are in quite a dilemma. I could not have asked for a better revenge. That's what you get, White-Rabbit." Dormouse lifted his leg to step on me. "Ah, you're already flat."

It was typical for Dormouse to lay on his face pounding the floor in a temper tantrum.

"So, you're hungry, huh?" he said, straightening his computer glasses and snapping at his suspenders, a sign the dormouse was temporarily sane. "Well, let's go to my mouse pad. I have a milk carton to show you."

Dormouse pushed and shoved me towards his hangout in the digital world, which was a rubber shack. He lifted a doormat, which read, *Not Welcome.* He picked up a brass key and shoved it into a keyhole. The keyhole squeaked open.

Tacked all over the walls were advertisement posters. There were ads for video games, comic strips, movies, clothing, cereal, and sports. The shack was a patchwork of magazine cutouts with no door, just a rusted keyhole.

"I'm hungry," I said.

"Pick any stain you want and lick."

There were soup, coffee, and mustard stains smeared all over. Fingerprints were smudged on the walls. There was a jagged hole in a corner with teeth marks.

"You're a slob, just like my brother," I noted.

"And you clean up your messes while hacking like a stupid girl."

Dormouse licked his whiskers, combing them with his paws. Shaking his rear, he walked to a table with crooked legs. A bread, cheese, and milk feast was laid out on top. There was one plate.

Dormouse tied a napkin around my neck. He squeezed tightly.

"You're choking me," I said, coughing.

"There is only one napkin," he said, glaring. He bent his chin to his chest and pointed to the back of his neck.

I untied the napkin from around my neck and wrapped the napkin around his neck. "I don't need a napkin to eat anyway. I don't make a mess," I muttered.

"Yeah, well you are in a mess." Dormouse poked the cheese loaf with a fork and a knife. He piled the slices on the plate. "You wouldn't like this cheese," he said, poking a chunk into his mouth. He chewed a mouthful while speaking. "This cheese is avatar cheese, not human cheese."

The voice was really coming from Dormouse's ten-year-old human creator who sat at his computer speaking through a microphone. If I was sitting at my computer controlling my avatar, White-Rabbit, I could take the food from him. It was awkward being a human paper doll inside a cyber world.

Dormouse lifted a milk carton to his lips, slurping the cream with his tongue.

The picture on the carton was of me! The gnomes had snapped my picture in the study. The gnomes then used the photo to let everyone know my human identity. On the milk carton, were the words: *Have you seen this hacker? The White-Rabbit, aka Jupiter, is on our most wanted list.* The ad then quoted my email address.

My body waved back and forth like an accordion. "Ah, music with Dory's meal. You do play a fearful tune, Jupiter. How did you get to be shaped like a musical instrument?" Dormouse ran his tongue around the milk carton rim.

What big trouble! Having my name, photograph, email address, and hacker handle blasted across the Internet was as serious as having my identity stolen. Even worse, if anyone ever posted to the world that I was a human digital girl, every greedy programmer would try to download me and turn me into an app.

"You look scared, Jupiter," Dormouse said and laughed.

I am scared! What will happen to me if I can't return home and become myself again, an ordinary human girl? If I ended up as an app on Google Play or the App Store, I would be lost forever in cyberspace!

B. Austin, Belinda Austin

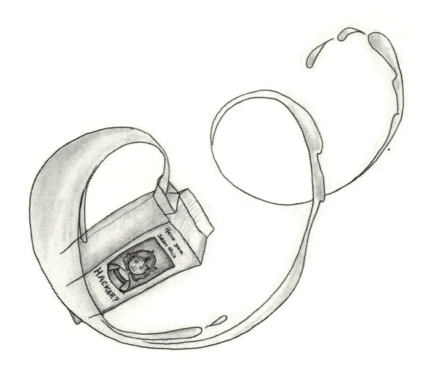

THE DORMOUSE GETS ME LOST

I flung my arm at the milk carton. The spout opened, pouring milk over my head. Like a wet paper doll, I folded to the floor, into a soaking pool of cream. My staircase folds straightened, proving Mom right—milk does build strong bones. Unfortunately, there was not enough milk left to beef up my muscles, so I was still flat, like a paper doll.

I shoved the milk carton, with my picture on it, under the table.

I picked at crumbs on the floor, stuffing them in my mouth and chewing silently. It took but a few crumbs to fill the stomach of a girl, tinier than a hummingbird.

My pocket was big enough to hold some crumbs of cheese for later.

Dormouse burped. He lifted his leg and farted, waving his hand around his rear end.

I held my nose.

"What? You think I stink?" he shouted. Dormouse threw his napkin on the floor and kicked the chair over.

He picked me up, sopping wet from milk.

Dormouse flung me from his pad.

I lay on the ground with my arms and legs twisted like pretzels, praying nothing tore.

"I kicked you out of my pad. Now you know what it feels like!" he screamed.

"You were voted out of the Nerds Computing Club, not kicked out. It was a Democratic process," I yelled.

"*It was a Democracy*," he mimicked. "They don't teach social studies in fifth grade!"

Dormouse grabbed my wrists, dragging me across a yellow brick road.

I was like a soggy sheet of paper. *Do not cry in front of Dormouse,* I thought. *Do not give the ten-year-old jerk the satisfaction! Chin up, Jupiter. Just be careful not to rip your arm. Soon, you will dry.*

Dormouse stopped at a sign that read, *Cable Station.*

We zigzagged through a maze of rainbow-colored tracks. At the end were three cable cars, a white car, a grey car, and a black car.

He lugged me into the grey cable car, slamming the door and locking us both in.

My damp body slid from the bench to the floor.

Dormouse placed his shoe on my chest.

The car twirled around, hanging us upside down.

The car flipped back around and my stomach flopped.

"Where are we going?" I said, trying not to sound fearful.

"This cable connects the monitor to the computer," he said.

I snapped my teeth, trying to bite his ankle.

He pinched my arm, causing a wrinkle on my soggy skin. Dormouse slumped against the seat but looked happy.

"If this cable car takes us into the computer's guts, do you know your way back up to the monitor?" I said.

"Why should I help you return when I can instead get you lost?" he laughed.

The cable car gave a jerk, and we started moving.

Like a roller coaster, the cable car went down, around and up in circles through a long, twisted cable.

It seemed my stomach moved to my ears before falling to my feet.

At last, the ride stopped and the doors opened.

I crawled from the cable car, moaning. My tummy felt like wires were stinging my intestines.

Dormouse spun dizzily on his tennis shoes. "We are inside the computer's guts. This is Cyber City where users in human forms are not welcome. This is the end of the line, Jupiter, and you crossed it. You broke the most major rule," he said, gloating.

I was too awestruck for ill humor. History might record that I was the first human to be physically inside a computer. Cyber City was a stunning mecca of flashing neon lights. The buildings were shiny metal and glass, reflecting colored lights bouncing off each other like a laser show. Cobalt-blue lights pulsed above the city, passing for a sky. In between crackling noises, a pleasant sound hummed like a fan blowing a cool breeze.

Taking the wrong cable car had not been such a bad idea. I no longer wished that the monitor was wireless. Dad's file labeled, *Irresponsible Jupiter*, was here, somewhere. An added benefit was that the wild ride in the twisted cable car acted like a spinning clothes dryer. I no longer walked like a wet dork but strutted with my chin held proudly.

Shadowy-like creatures kept bumping into us without even a how-do-you-do or a pardon-me. They were avatars that moved quickly, except for the occasional avatar that stopped for a microsecond to examine me.

One avatar moved in a menacing way.

The avatar pounced, causing me to shriek.

Dormouse grabbed me by the collar and yanked me up a building.

I clung to his shoe and stuck out my tongue at the avatar below.

The walls were loose, and flapped as we climbed, causing the buildings to sway. What a relief to be away from those menacing shadows.

Dormouse climbed through a window of the 13th floor and knocked on a glass door with the name, *Computer File Room*. No one answered. He turned the handle, clicking his teeth nervously as he swung the door open.

Trees sprouted in the room like a forest. Instead of leaves hanging from the branches, manila file folders dangled. Each file-tree had a name.

Books lined the walls, but the books were untouchable. Instead, my hand sunk into the wall. "These aren't real books, just pictures," I said, snorting. "Are there any hard walls in Cyber City?"

"Just wallpaper hangs between the rooms, for pretty," he said.

Files hung from the branches of a file-tree. I snapped off a folder with a label *Backup*. There were four envelopes in this heavy folder. Consequently, I emptied parts of the folder into the trashcan before hanging the folder back on its file tree, since none of the files was of interest.

I kept picking off files, sorting through the contents and emptying some in the can. "I hope those weren't important," I mumbled. A file named *Recovery* lay atop the trash heap.

Bingo! *Irresponsible Jupiter* was stamped on the label of a folder that drooped from a branch on the next tree.

I broke off the folder with care, and hugged it. "Mission accomplished. We can go now."

"Go where, flathead?" Dormouse said.

"Back up to the monitor, cheese brain."

He scratched his head. "Well if I'm a cheese brain, I have too many holes in my skull so, I can't remember the way back," he yelled.

"You are so not cool!" I hollered, boxing his nose.

Dormouse punched back with his bigger paws. He knocked me to the floor and stood over me, wiggling his whiskers.

"Getting us lost in the computer is flipping me out," I said.

"I am not lost, but you are a helpless fool without your avatar," Dormouse said.

He dug his claws into the wood of the desk and climbed with me dangling from one of his suspenders. With my other hand, I hugged the file to my chest.

Dormouse heaved us onto the desktop.

On the desktop was a winter wonderland. There was a dark-blue sky with white balls hanging above thick snow. A snow-cone forest rose from the white ground.

Dormouse slid in the frozen snow. He tripped and knocked over an inkbottle. He hopped on one foot. "Gosh, darn!" He plopped down and ripped off his tennis shoe and sock. He clipped his toenail with his teeth, ripping away the jagged edges. He licked around his trimmed toenail to sand his nail smooth with his rough tongue.

Meanwhile, ink kept spilling from the bottle he had turned topsy-turvy. I tried to lift the bottle, but it was too heavy. I attempted to shove the cap on the bottle to stop the spill, but the bottle kept rolling. The dripping ink made the desktop resemble blue ice.

I wiped at the ink spot on the desktop with a tissue, but the spot got bigger. "Oh, well, an ink blot is like yesterday's newspaper," I said, tossing the tissue over my shoulder.

Bingo! The desktop was the *graphical user interface* or *GUI* for the computer. My way home was hidden in the link between my world and the cyber world, the desktop. *There must be a help menu*, I thought.

"You don't remember where you left things on the desktop!" I shouted.

"Yes, I do." Dormouse scurried to the other side of the desk and dived into a trashcan. He dug in the trash, stuffing a half-eaten slice of spam in his mouth.

"Help me find the *help menu*, Dormouse," I yelled down the trashcan.

The little turd threw a birdie.

How dare he throw a dirty finger, I thought. Huffing and puffing, I pushed a giant eraser across the desktop and over the side of the desk. The eraser landed dead center in the trashcan.

Dormouse cursed until the last thing to be erased was his obnoxious mouth.

A DICTIONARY NAMED MERRIAM

There must be a *help menu* somewhere on the desktop. Eureka! Under the snow was a basket marked, *Out*

Email. I scribbled a letter on a scrap of paper. The letter read:

Dear Dad, please do not be angry. I am lost inside your computer and have become a digital girl. It is not my fault that the computer Gnomes kidnapped me.

Love,

Your so responsible daughter, Jupiter

I underlined the words, <u>so responsible</u>, with the color red and then dropped the letter in the Out-Email basket.

Ping!

A yellow envelope addressed to *Jupiter* popped into the In-Email Basket. The sender cut each letter of my name from a magazine and glued the letters on crookedly. My heart skipped at the thought that this must be a blackmail email since the letter was addressed to my real name. Dormouse's toenail made a great letter opener. The email had two sentences: We no who u r. We have been watching u.

"Whoever you are, you need a spell checker," I bellowed. The email fit in my small pocket.

Computer hackers were lousy spellers because we wrote in scripting languages to break into computers. The Internet was a secret tunnel to dig our way through, one keyboard stroke at a time. We wrote script programs to run as fast as lightning, guessing at passwords. We stole the login names or deduced the login from stolen files. Oops, I meant borrowed files.

"I would give anything for a dictionary," I hollered.

Presto, a dictionary emerged in the file room. "Maid Merriam here, unabridged dictionary." Maid Merriam was dressed rather smartly in white shoes, white gloves, and a top hat.

"What is the formal meaning of ir-res-pon-si-ble?" I said, pronouncing each syllable.

Her gold-leaf pages flapped as the dictionary spoke in a fluttery voice. "First, hand over your ballet shoes."

"These are dancing shoes, you know-it-all book."

"We shall play Scrabble for your shoes then," Merriam said.

"I am not stupid enough to play Scrabble with a dictionary."

"Perhaps you are mad enough then. My top hat, I won it playing Scrabble with a mad hatter."

"Just do your job and define the word *irresponsible*."

"You said, you would give anything for my help," Merriam said.

I grabbed the dictionary around her middle, trying to turn her pages.

Merriam kicked and slapped.

I forced her pages open to the letter **I**.

Merriam snapped her book cover closed. The dictionary stood in a fighting pose with her pages open to the word, *karate*. Her hands changed to boxing gloves.

"Give me the meaning of *irresponsible*, or I'll find matches for a book burning party!"

"Tut, tut, child! Every word has a definition, if only you can find it."

I grabbed her back and front covers, trying to pry her open.

Merriam kept her spine clamped shut.

"First, your shoes," she said, snapping her fingers.

I removed the ballet shoes from around my neck and handed the pair to Merriam.

The dictionary did have legs and feet. She twirled on my ballet shoes. "How do I look?"

"Like a silly romance novel."

"I am not a silly romance, although an encyclopedia did break my heart last year."

"If you wanted a pair of ballet shoes, why not just remove a pair from your pages?" I said.

"Because I wanted your shoes to see if you could dance, but you are a clumsy dancer," she said and tripped on my shoes.

"I fulfilled my part of our bargain," I said. "Now define *irresponsible* for me."

"I refuse to help a silly dancer. Silly! Silly!" she screamed.

I shoved Merriam.

The dictionary fell sideways on the snowy desktop. She kicked her legs like a bug turned upside down. The dictionary was open to the letter R. "Quick! Help me to right myself, before *rhyme* and *reason* escape my pages," she shrieked.

Merriam was heavy from the weight of every English word. Nevertheless, I pushed the dictionary back on its legs. "Is *thank you* defined in your pages?" I said, glaring.

"Phrases are not," Merriam said. She fluttered to the letter i. "Irresponsible means, not being responsible," she said, spitting ink from her pages.

"What is the use in defining all of that stuff, if you don't explain it as you go on? *Irresponsible* is by far the most confusing word ever defined," I said.

"Well then, we must dig for the word's root and find a better definition," she said. Merriam flapped her pages to the letter R. "*Responsible* means, being to blame for something as in, who is responsible for deleting Louse-the-Mouse and the hacker known as Dormouse?"

"You're making the examples up about the mouses! According to your definition of *responsible*, I can't be *irresponsible*, because I am *responsible* for erasing Dormouse, who erased Louse-the-Mouse," I said, sniffling.

She flipped her pages to the letter *K*. "Well in that case, *karma* is responsible for erasing Dormouse, who erased Louse-the-Mouse, which means that you are *irresponsible* Jupiter."

"What are you writing on the i page and how do you know my name?" I shrieked.

"How I know your name is a secret; and you're welcome for making you famous. All of the online dictionaries will now use the hacker Jupiter as an example of *irresponsible*."

"No," I screamed. "I must prove that I'm responsible!"

"Ta-ta then, and break a leg!" Merriam waved her pinky.

"Do not leave me stranded here. There must be some word in your dictionary that can help me return home."

"I am late for a beauty pageant which is why I needed to learn ballet." Merriam twirled clumsily on my slippers. "Goodbye, human, digital girl, stupid user, bad dancer, avatar, gnome hunter, cheater, nerd, hacker, whatever you are. My adjectives are arguing over what kind of creature you are." She placed a hand on my head, as if bestowing a title. "I declare you a *bicycle*, due to that tire around your middle."

I pushed her.

Merriam lost her balance. She toppled into the file trees.

There was a noise from the desktop. The snow cones moved.

"Eek! Gnomes," Merriam screamed.

The snow cones stood, revealing legs. The gnomes had been hiding beneath the snow cones.

The dictionary fluttered its pages, throwing nouns, mainly pots, pans, plates, saucers, and a Scrabble Game at the gnomes.

Pouf! The dictionary vanished.

The gnomes ran on their pointy shoes, slipping and sliding. The beasties resembled Santa's elves dressed in red and green sticky-note snowsuits held together with paper clips. Even though the gnomes had doubled up the sticky-notes for warmth, their shiny lips froze to their snowy moustaches. They grinned with vampire-like teeth.

Snow flew everywhere, unburying a map. The map had a C Drive, D Drive, E Drive and other letters. Even better, a square on the map read, HOME.

Flying gnomes sang repeatedly, "March on the right path and by March, you will have marched so far, you will be marching back the way you came."

It was April, and March was eleven months away! There must be a shortcut. "Which road is the right path to HOME?" I said, biting my nails. "Oh, the gnomes are getting closer!"

The map resembled a flat Monopoly game token. I jumped on a square that read STARTUP, and then screamed when the square moved towards a square named SHUTDOWN. I backed away from SHUTDOWN, but STARTUP changed directions, hovering in the air next to a brick labeled RESTART.

Eek! Gnomes chopped off five bricks on one of the paths towards HOME.

Each time I ran down a path, gnomes hacked the squares in half with teensy-weensy snow shovels, while singing.

Gnomes chopped off every path until HOME floated on an iceberg, out of my reach. The gnomes then vanished.

Surrounding the iceberg were snow cones, as if the gnomes never revealed themselves.

I RIDE A TROJAN HORSE

It sounded like heavy boots moving towards the room. Someone yelled out in a German accent, "We are coming for you, White-Rabbit! I mean, Jupiter!"

I tripped on the *Help* key of a calculator, slid on its *Backspace* key, and tumbled off the desktop. I bounced on a leaf pile in the trashcan, flew up, and landed on the floor.

The door handle slowly turned.

I pushed the swinging door on a file-tree with a name tag, *Garden*, and walked into a cool, spring scene. This room was made of wallpaper with sunflowers, daisies, and multi-colored roses growing on the walls.

I climbed to the bluest daisy and plopped down in the middle of the flower. "The difference between me and these flowers is that they will bloom next spring, whereas I..."

A Cuckoo Bumblebee hovered in front of my nose. Some Cuckoos lived in New Mexico and California, but this Cuckoo had not heard the war was over. The bee wore red flying goggles and a brown, World-War-I-leather flying cap. The bee rakishly flung an orange scarf around its neck. Its antennas were wires. Its wings were a rainbow's colors, with sparks of light when it fluttered about. The bee had two fangs, from which yellow goo dripped. It buzzed with a thick lisp against my ear.

The Cuckoo twirled through the air, spelling words like an airplane. *Your pollen tastes yucky*, the bee spelled.

"That's not pollen in my ear; it's earwax."

The bee sucked on my cheek and then spelled, *U r an odd flour. Your pollen tastes salty.*

"Those are my tears you've tasted, you Cuckoo Bumblebee. Go away, and leave me alone!"

Bye jovey! U r a daisy, it spelled. The bee slapped its forehead with its metal arm. A dent was between its hundreds of eyes.

"I'm not a daisy. I'm an Jupiter."

Jupiter, the sour-tasting flour, it spelled.

"And you are Cuckoo, the bumbler bee who cannot spell."

Know. U r wrong. Eye am a spelling bee, the bee said, drawing flashy words in the air. *Eye nose how too spell reel good. Eye bee a spill chequer, 2 catch a user miss steaks. Weather Eye am write oar wrong, rarely dew eye maid mist aches.*

"Well, I have often seen a spelling bee; but a bee spelling? You have spelled wordless sentences. Are you a hacker?" I said suspiciously because Bumbler could not spell.

I help u, Cuckoo spelled, spinning somersaults in the air.

"Show-off," I said and smiled.

The bee hung upside down, flapping its wings. It pointed at the window with one antenna.

"Oh, alright." I jumped off the daisy and followed Cuckoo to the window.

The bee banged its nose against the glass. "Bzz. Bz. Z." It crashed to the floor appearing unconscious.

The Cuckoo was a spell checker for the computer and therefore, a program. "Program crash. Restart," I yelled, counting, "One. Two. Three."

"Z. Bz. Bzz." Cuckoo flew around the room and then once more, banged its nose on the glass.

"Get out, pest," I said, opening the window.

Cuckoo flew out the window, landing on the ear of a wooden horse, whose head reached the 13th floor window.

In Greek Mythology, the Trojans used a similar, giant wooden horse to rescue a beautiful girl.

I grabbed onto the horse's ears and slid down its neck, bouncing on the saddle. I was a pocket-sized girl on a massive horse, hoping to look more lovely than nerdy.

The wooden horse turned its head and winked.

"Are you a Trojan horse?" I said.

"I'm a sick Trojan," it said through stiff lips, sounding like a cowboy.

"I'm homesick myself," I said.

"I'm not sick of home. I just carry a virus," the Trojan said.

"I'm homesick for the real world. You're so pretty," I said, patting his mane. "We must find you a virtual veterinarian to cure your virus."

The Trojan whinnied, rolling down the street on wooden, squealing wheels.

Cuckoo flew from the horse's ear landing, stinger down, on its rump.

The Trojan hollered, spinning its wheels down the street at high speed.

"Yi," I yelled, slipping and grabbing onto a rope hanging from the saddle.

The rope gave way and the wooden horse's hollow belly snapped open. A pack of chariots zoomed from its stomach. On each chariot rode a gnome, buggy-red-eyed, with sharp teeth and runny nose. The gnomes were dressed like Trojan warriors with feathered helmets, red skirts, and capes. Sandals crisscrossed their short legs. They held their shields in front of them, waving their swords and screaming, "Bloody war!"

The Trojan-gnomes paid no attention to me. They all stared intently ahead, like gnomes on a mission.

A pack of fleas flew behind the gnomes. Their wings were long. The fleas let off a powerful stench as they flew in formation, like bomber planes, in the direction of *Cyber City*.

The Trojan-gnomes snapped their whips at the chariots to fly faster until the gnomes and fleas became mere specks in the sky.

The Trojan belched, feeling better now that its nasty stomachache had flown from its belly.

The horse wheeled away with me still swinging from the rope.

My arms were weakening. There was about a thirteen-story drop to the ground.

Cuckoo lifted its stinger from the rump of the Trojan horse.

The horse swished its tail at a gang of fleas on its back.

A flea fell on Cuckoo. "Bzzzzzz," the bee hissed.

The flea flew away with a bit of Cuckoo hanging from its mouth.

Cuckoo brushed its wings against my leg.

"Stop or you'll make me let go of this rope. I shall break my digital head then. Spell, *escape this mess*," I said, kicking at the bee.

The stubborn Cuckoo hovered beneath me, until I wrapped my legs around its back. The bee's body felt furry soft. Its wire antennas vibrated in my hands.

We flew through the Trojan's legs whose wheels were screeching downhill.

A MAD, MAD JAVA PARTY

Cuckoo flew into a cloud, shaped like a coffee pot. We poured from the cloud's spout, through a flowered archway, and into a garden surrounded by a white picket fence. Singing birds perched on statues. Rainbows shot from fountains. Except for holes littering the garden, this place looked like a paradise.

Incoming, Cuckoo spelled with wiggly lines, before skidding to a stop on a table. The bee banged its antennas against a coffee pot labeled, *Java Virtual Machine*. The machine churned away, Java spitting from the spigot. Java was the most powerful programming language. Java trickled across the table, staining the tablecloth black.

Identical twins, with block-shaped heads, hunkered at the head of the party table. They dressed alike, with high starched collars and choking, bow ties. Their beady eyes hid behind wire-rimmed glasses. Their names were sewn proudly on tweed jackets. The twins had enormous ears and were identical, except for two differences. One twin had his head screwed on backward. His name was *Illogic*. His brother's name was *Logic*. Logic smoked a pipe, but Illogic had a pipe sticking out of his left ear, dripping with earwax.

"Well, Cuckoo, we see you have arrived with your usual, clumsy flair," Logic said.

"Exception," Illogic screamed. "You have arrived with your usual fare, Cuckoo! Cuckoo! Cuckoo!" Illogic slapped himself. "There is no fare; the Java party is free. Not free! Flee," he shrieked in a panicked voice. Illogic whipped his head back, flinging his chair over. He wrestled with his legs to keep them from running away.

"My brother tried to divide by zero too many times," Logic explained. He switched his brother's full cup of Java, with his own empty cup. Logic sipped the Java, rattling the cup against the saucer. His head twitched. Like his brother, his face was long and thin. His crew-cut hairstyle shaped his head like a block.

"I knew it! Blockheads," I said.

"We are heads of the block, and we did not invite you to our block party, daisy," Logic said.

"Like I told Cuckoo, I am not a daisy," I said.

"*Like I told Cuckoo, I am not a daisy*," Logic mimicked. "Then go, Daisy. We only allow artificial intelligence at our party."

"Then why is a block of wood here?" I said.

"Because this is a block party," Illogic screeched.

The block of wood wore a baseball cap. It was a lump of bocote wood with streaks, creating a lizard-like face. It had swirls of eyes at each top corner and a bump centered at the top. The block of wood resembled an earless Yoda with wrinkles of woody lines.

"The block of wood is a block of programming code. Blocky is a great thinker," Logic added.

Blocky spoke with an Australian accent. "How ya goin', Mates? No smokin' allowed or matches. We want no fires. G'day, Mates," it said. Glue dribbled from cracks in its wood.

Logic puffed on his pipe, swirling smoke around Blocky.

The block of wood coughed.

"If Blocky's words are so wise, why don't you follow the wood's advice and not smoke?" I said.

"I don't smoke. My pipe smokes." Logic placed his pipe to rest on Blocky. The pipe glowed red.

Illogic smacked my hand away from the cookie jar. "Exception! As you can see, there is not enough food. Yuck. Yuck," he said.

"Why, there's enough food to feed an army," I said.

"There is enough food to feed an army," Illogic said. He snapped his fingers, and ants parachuted from the sky. Hundreds of ants landed on the table. The ants wore army helmets and four pairs of combat boots. One ant played the trumpet, and another ant played the drums. The ants resembled plain red ants, except that the ants had snouts like pigs.

The ants marched in tune, toward the food.

"The picnic is for the army ants," Illogic said.

"Giving a picnic for ants is a harebrained idea," I said.

Logic wagged his finger. "Tut-tut. This ant army is the anti-virus, programmed to fight the computer virus that has infected the world. The army will march off in a WAR file. Combat is their program."

"This may be their last meal," Illogic said.

An ant, with four plastic stars glued to its helmet, clicked its combat boots together. "We are ready to attack, and await your orders," the ant said, saluting Logic.

"Go ahead, General Ant, the feast is all yours," Logic said, saluting the ant back.

The ants sounded like pigs as their snout noses moved through the food like vacuum cleaners.

Cuckoo buzzed around the table, dipping into Java cups. The black stuff dripped from its fangs, staining his scarf.

Logic poked my back with a fork, scooting me to the end of the table where sat a big-bellied beetle, dressed in a fancy pinstriped suit.

"Quit stabbing me with your fork!" I yelled.

Logic spoke with his thin nose in the air with a snotty, British accent. "If you must stay, then be seated. We sit from the head to the foot of the table, according to class. You may be seated at the lowest end, Daisy."

"Stop calling me lower class, you freaky avatar! I'm not a daisy," I said, kicking the table.

The beetle winked. "And I'm not an avatar. I'm a software bug. None of us is avatars at this table, including you. Trust me to keep my mouth shut, User." The bug spoke through the side of its mouth, like a gangster. A cigar hung from its lip. Like Cuckoo, its antennas were wires, but bent. Its legs were created from hairy wires. The hair on its legs gave off flashes of colored light.

"Do I look so much like a user?" I said in a small voice.

"You've got that lost face about you, like you're overwhelmed by technology," the bug said.

"Oh, but I'm a..."

"Hacker? I know," the bug said and farted. "Being a hacker ain't the same thing as being digital."

"I appear lost because this is my first time as a digital girl, inside the computer. None of you like users?" I whispered.

The bug leaned back in its chair and smiled lazily, puffing on a cigar. "Envy often leads to dislike, don't it? You and I have more in common than you think."

"I have nothing in common with a computer bug," I said.

"A single program does not limit you and me, as it does them." The bug pointed its antennae to the others at the Java party. A figure appearing like the Grim Reaper reclined on the right side of the table. She wore a raggedy-hooded, black robe, and black mask. A teensy man sat opposite Grim Reaper. The tiny man had a huge, balloon-head attached to a long, spaghetti-neck.

"Hopefully she won't lose her temper," I said, eyeing the blood-specked scythe. Grim Reaper's face was just a shadow with eyes. She cursed when she tried to eat a cookie.

Stinky said, "Ignore Grim Reaper and her bad temper. The Reaper is berserk because she will never drink a cup of Java because she has no mouth. Her job is executions in the *City of Memory Chips*."

I raised an eyebrow at the tiny man with the heart-shaped balloon-head, waving about his threadlike neck. The balloon head was transparent pink, displaying a pea-sized brain.

"That is just Oxy-Moron, a thesaurus. The virus killed off all his synonyms and left the antonyms."

Oxy-Moron tried to drink warm water, but a breeze blew his head about the glass. He raised a glass with his tiny hands. "Let us toast to our affluent poverty!" His balloon head jiggled like a car dashboard figure with a springy neck. "Thank you for calling, and have a nice day," he said in an East Indian customer-service voice.

"Can you help me?" I whispered to Stinky.

"Bugs only help themselves," the bug said.

"They're crazy," I said, pointing my chin to the twins.

"We're all mad here. This place has become an insane asylum since the virus," Stinky said.

"Everyone's fighting over cups of Java, yet there's plenty to go around."

"Human beings are made up of 70% water. The smartest cyber-beings are programmed with 100% Java," Stinky said.

The bug jumped on the table and stood upright like a human. It balanced on the longest two of its six spaghetti legs. The bug rubbed its antennas together. The beetle's natural pinstriped suit transformed to a formal tuxedo. Even dressed in a silk top hat, white tie, and tails, the beetle was gross with bags puffed beneath its eyes. Its face was flushed grey, with blisters and boils covering its skin. A jagged knife scar cut its face in half. The bug did have a wonderful voice though. The beetle tap-danced across the table, swinging a golden cane beneath its arm, and singing.

"I want a lazy programmer,

No error checking so the program I can freeze.

Give me a hazy programmer,

One who cannot see the forest for the trees.

Oh, where is the crazy programmer?

One with no logic, please."

The bug leaned on its cane, tipped the silk hat, and bowed.

"Oh, that is funny," I said, clapping.

The bug farted and laughed at me while I buried my nose in a napkin. "My breakfast smells good, don't it? I ate part of a program that spits out a recipe for boiled eggs," the bug said. "I'm originally from a malicious program and have the code to be destructive."

"Stinky," I said, pinching my nose.

The bug shook its fist and snarled, "How do you know my name? Did Moles snitch?"

"Moles do not confide in me. I never use a Mole for hacking. I am not a friend of Moles, but I'm your friend, Stinky," I said, smiling and lying. A computer bug might be useful.

"Good cause I wanna be your friend. A user with hacking skills could come in handy. You and I could be soulmates." Stinky rubbed my leg with its creepy antennae. The bug's eyes turned all soft and mushy.

I never had a boyfriend before, but I once had a crush on the hacker Zebra. I admired big horsey teeth. Now, a bug was attracted to me. Antennas in a boyfriend were a big turnoff so, I slapped the bug's antenna from my thigh and changed the subject from romance. "Speaking of Moles, what is that one doing here," I whispered and pointed. Moles usually attacked the Internet instead of personal computers, yet a Mole ran past us in a hurry.

Stinky said, "I ain't afraid of moles. I covered my tracks with so much spaghetti code, no hacker will ever exploit me with a Mole, or Worm, or anything else."

The Mole circled and came back. The avatar of a hacker who goes by the handle Hedgehog joined the Mole. Hedgehog used to be a member of Nerds Computing Club but believed we were not creating enough chaos so he quit the club.

Stinky burped, rubbing its big belly. "It's that heartburn program I took a byte out of yesterday. A heart doesn't agree with me, White-Rabbit, so don't ever think this thing between us is love."

The bug said my hacker handle, while Hedgehog spoke into a cellphone! Hedgehog was only eleven but he left Nerds Computing Club and went over to the dark side of the web. He hung out in bad areas of the Internet at trashy online clubs. Ghost hackers recruited the kid. The specialty of a ghost hacker was to utilize Moles to burrow through a user's web browser while the user surfed the Internet. If your computer ever got infected with a virus after you surfed a web page, it was probably a ghost hacker.

While Hedgehog spoke on the phone, the Mole ran in circles again as if it was agitated. A RAT jogged with the Mole. A RAT was sometimes used by hackers to steal email addresses. For example, with a RAT, a person could be sitting in Iowa and control someone's computer who was in New York, just by using an email address.

What exactly was Hedgehog up to with a Mole and a RAT?

B. Austin, Belinda Austin

I DANCE FOR MY SUPPER

The twin, Illogic, dug a hole in the garden, muttering something about, "gnome treasure." He threw dirt on the table across the food. His pants had quite a few byte marks on the cloth. A piece of cloth, the same color, hung from the bug's mouth.

The beetle chewed, swallowed, and burped. "I promise not to tell your secret about being a human. Honor amongst crooks," Stinky said.

"I'm not a crook," I hissed.

"Ain't you? Breaking and entering? Rubbing out Louse?"

"Dormouse rubbed out Louse."

"And what happened to Dormouse?" The bug posed an antenna in a question mark.

"Shush! I didn't know the eraser would, well, you know."

"Oh, cripes, you rubbed out your navigator." The bug laughed so hard that tears ran down its cheeks.

Illogic plopped down between us. Illogic and Stinky put their heads together and spoke softly. "The daisy looks too familiar," Illogic said.

"Her face is on a milk carton," Stinky added.

"She is a saltine." Illogic slapped his head.

"I am not a cracker," I yelled. "I'm a hacker!"

"Shut up, saltine!" Illogic said in a shrill voice. "You cracker your way in here. You cracker your way into soup. Someone, bring me a straw to drink this soda cracker!" Illogic poked my head with a straw. He slurped a few strands of my hair.

"That hurts! I hope you choke."

Illogic pinched me and snarled, "You are not a very nice daisy."

"What's the reward for a cracker these days?" Stinky said.

"Becoming an icon on the desktop," Illogic said.

Stinky pounded a claw on the table. "I need to be an icon on the computer screen, so users can click on my pretty face, and break their programs. I gotta win that reward, before the Gnome King gets her."

"What Gnome King?" I said and gulped.

Illogic said, "I'll split the reward with you, Stinky. We will get a scam going. No! A spam! We will use email to spam that the computer has been crackered! I have crackered up! They're coming to take me away to the crazy house!" Illogic hugged his legs that were furiously kicking the air, trying to escape.

A pounding noise came from carpenter ants, who were building a stage.

Logic snapped his fingers, and a microphone rose in his hand. His clothes changed to a white tuxedo. "Before we entertain the troops, who are to battle the virus, I'll loosen up the crowd with a joke. What is the last line written in the User Manual?"

"Customer support's phone number and a credit card number request," I yelled.

"What is the last line written in the user Manual?" Logic repeated and pointed to his brother.

"In case of an emergency landing, your laptop can be used as a flotation device!" Illogic said.

"Correct! My brother wins the door prize, again. Another pig."

Presto! The block of wood changed into a pig.

Logic rocked the pig like a baby, and then threw the pig at his brother.

Illogic caught the snorting pig. He dumped a gallon of pepper on the pig. "Pepper for the pig! More pepper!" he shouted. "We must season the main course!"

"Should we season the pig with summer, winter, spring, or fall?" Stinky yelled.

"Beat the pig, if it sneezes," Grim Reaper snarled, pounding the scythe on the ground.

The shaking earth woke some caterpillars, who slinked from their garden beds. One caterpillar sat on the pig. The caterpillar wore a straw hat shading it from the sun.

Suddenly, a message appeared written in smoke: LOOK FOR ME!

I spun around but could see no friendly face.

A caterpillar crawled up my arm. This caterpillar wore computer glasses and smoked a hookah pipe. His big nose kept his owl-like glasses from falling off his face.

"Oh, it's you," I whispered back with huge relief.

My hacker friend Caterpillar sat on my shoulder and took a puff of his pipe. "I was waiting for an opportunity to hack in. Hello, White-Rabbit," he whispered in a voice sounding wise, like Yoda from *Star Wars*. Indeed, Caterpillar hummed the theme song from the movie.

"Hello," I said. Here was rescue, at last. It took all my control not to kiss Caterpillar, but that would be weird.

"I have something important to say," he said. Caterpillar cleared his throat of a few clods of dirt. "Keep your temper, or else you might lose your head," he said, very businesslike.

"Is that all you have to say?" I squeaked.

"No. You received an email earlier," Caterpillar said, puffing on his pipe.

"That was you?"

"No," Caterpillar said, blowing smoke in my face.

"Then what?" I said, coughing.

Thinking always caused wrinkles on Caterpillar's face to deepen. "There was something important. Ah, yes. What could you do with an email and a RAT?"

"I could gain control of a computer and all its peripherals, such as the camera and speakers," I said.

"What computer could you gain control of?"

"With the email in my pocket addressed to me, and a Remote Administration Tool (RAT), I could gain control of this computer. Did you send the RAT to help me?"

"No, but what is the probability of a RAT, a Mole and Hedgehog being together at a Java party?"

"Hedgehog must be up to no good again. If I am to get the RAT's help, the hard part will be enticing the RAT to abandon Hedgehog," I said.

Caterpillar's voice suddenly changed from wise, ancient Yoda to a boy. "Oops! Sorry, but I have no more time to solve your problems. My mom is calling me for breakfast. We are going out of town to visit an aunt who lives in the mountains with no Internet access. I got a dirt bike yesterday for my 13th birthday. If you ever get out of this mess, maybe we can take another online vacation. We should race cars over the Swiss Alps."

"Neat!"

"Bye, Jupiter. Nice knowing who you really are."

"Wait! You know my real name. What is *your* real name?" I said to the air.

"Ah, now that is a riddle," Caterpillar said, leaving behind some smoke in the shape of a question mark.

There were two worms staring at the stage, and then four, and then eight worms, etc. The worms were duplicating themselves. These were worms created by a hacker.

The worms crawled away, no doubt headed for a network of computers, so each could infect one.

One worm stayed behind.

My friend Caterpillar reappeared on my shoulder. "I forgot to remove the worm I used to hack into the computer," he said.

Ping! Caterpillar and the lone worm vanished before I could even wish Caterpillar a nice vacation biking down the mountains.

"And now, for what you've all been waiting for, the entertainment!" Logic yanked open purple, velvet curtains which hung on the stage.

How odd, the stage is a jewelry box. There is even a mirror, I thought.

The spotlight moved from the empty stage, to me. "You must entertain us, daisy." The twins pushed me up the steps to the jewelry box.

"But the dictionary has my ballet slippers!" I objected.

"Break a leg!" they all yelled.

"Break your right leg," Logic added.

"Break your wrong leg," Illogic said.

Everyone sat stiffly eying the stage through binoculars, even Grim Reaper.

"Play the music to *Swan Lake*," I said in a voice filled with stage fright.

"You may not use helper programs, cheater," the twins hollered.

With one foot wobbling against my leg, I balanced on the toe of my tennis shoe. I lifted my hands above my head, posing like a ballerina doll in my favorite jewelry box. However, my flattened body resembled a ballet paper doll—the amazing digital girl, dancer extraordinaire.

I twisted my hands high and spun. It was odd twirling on the toe of my sneaker to no music. I imagined dancing on a grand stage, with my family sitting in the audience.

Poof! I toppled and landed on my butt. Ouch! The audience threw flowerless, thorny stems. There were murmurs about "program crashes," "bugs," and "drink more Java."

"It's not my fault! I've never practiced on a spinning stage. I am a trooper though, and the show must go on." I lifted my trembling chin, and stood like a statue. A haunting tune played, and the disk turned.

The song suddenly changed to an old Frank Sinatra tune. "Call me irresponsible. Call me unreliable. Throw in undependable, too..."

The disk quit turning, and hurled me from the stage. I landed next to the *Java Virtual Machine*, banging my head.

"That performance doesn't deserve supper," Logic said.

"Her legs are weak since she hasn't eaten," Stinky yelled from the audience.

"Let her eat cake then," Illogic ordered.

Grim Reaper and Stinky each grabbed me by an arm. They dragged me to the table, plopping me down on a chair.

Logic banged a cake plate against the table. A note leaned against a slice of carrot cake. The note read, *laced with irresponsibility. Eat me.*

"Never!" I cried.

Grim Reaper and Stinky both held me down, while the twins force-fed me every letter of the word *irresponsibility*.

I vomited the letters *i* and *r*, which just left *responsibility* in my stomach. An enormous burp erupted from my mouth. "Excuse me, but *responsibility* disagrees with me."

They all threw their cups and saucers, shouting, "You are very funny, Jupiter, though you have no humor."

Oxy-Moron shouted, "Friendly-fire approaches."

It was the nasty fleas and Trojan-gnomes flying over the Java party, in bomber formation.

The Trojan-gnomes leaned over their chariots, throwing green-slime bombs. They struck Logic and he collapsed, next to a pile of party favors.

The army ants fired their weapons, but were no match for the fleas and Trojan-gnomes.

Grim Reaper, Illogic and Stinky, were the only ones left dancing on the table. Illogic danced a do-si-do with Stinky. Grim Reaper jumped with the Java Beans and army ants.

Trojan-gnomes parachuted from their chariots, the beasties joining the party. They performed a dance, kicking their sandals and twirling shields.

The RAT? Where is the RAT? Ah, there it is, making its escape with the Mole.

The virus struck Hedgehog and he vanished.

The hacker, whose avatar Hedgehog represented, likely rebooted his computer, hoping to be in time to rejoin the Mole and RAT who were making their escape in a rowboat.

A hand yanked a carrot from the cake, including the roots and dirt. "Hello, Jupiter. Caterpillar sent me to help," a voice said, followed by the sound of a crunching carrot.

I turned and looked into the face of my avatar, White-Rabbit.

AN AVATAR HELPS ME

White-Rabbit said, "Do you like my outfit? My purse matches my bow and eyeglasses." The look in her eyes said I had better compliment her or else.

"You look lovely," I hastily said, smiling brightly. The RAT was going to get away, but White-Rabbit insisted on showing off her clothes and listing all of the designers. She wore a dark grey dress with black polka dots, a white color and cuffs, and a white ruffled tie. Her face was a bespectacled, floppy-eared rabbit but the rest of her resembled my arms and legs.

"The RAT and the Mole are up to no good," I mumbled.

"Yes," White-Rabbit said, rotating her eyes while keeping her face foreword. Like a real rabbit, she could see in a near-complete circle, except for one blind spot in front of her nose. Therefore, White-Rabbit could see behind her. White-Rabbit had a very good security system and was very useful for hacking.

She wiggled her nose disapprovingly. "The RAT's pants are torn and stained. It's dressed like a beggar in that baggy sweater!"

"Well, it is a RAT, after all."

"You have no fashion sense. Try to keep up!" White-Rabbit hopped across the fields chasing the RAT and Mole.

It was an odd relationship, me not being in control of White-Rabbit with a mouse or joystick. My avatar was telling me what to do.

Suddenly, the ground shook with a powerful thumping of t-strapped dress shoes. White-Rabbit had found her prey. White-Rabbit hid behind a bend of electrical wires. The bunny stood frozen, watching the Mole digging a hole. The freezing was bunny behavior at the sight of danger.

"The mole is letting another RAT into the computer," White-Rabbit whispered.

A smaller RAT climbed out of the hole the Mole was digging.

"The Mole has itty-bitty eyes hidden by its fur. It's a European Mole," I noted, "so the Mole has photopic vision. It's so bright in here from all the neon lights that the Mole might see us."

White-Rabbit snapped open a parasol matching her purse. "Here. I'll distract the Mole and then you shade the light to blind it with this parasol."

"Moles hear at low frequencies," I said.

Luckily, the Mole's digging was making a lot of noise so the Mole did not hear us sneak up on it. We stretched our necks to make sure we were not low to the ground where Moles hear the best.

White-Rabbit tapped the Mole on its back. "You have decent shoes, but you should at least wear pants," she said.

I lifted the parasol, shading the Mole from the light.

"Who's there?" The Mole held out its hands like a blind person.

At the speed of a blink, White-Rabbit kicked the Mole in the hole.

I quickly threw dirt in the hole, burying the Mole.

While I chased the smaller RAT, White-Rabbit surprised the large RAT who was sleeping.

The big RAT growled and gnashed its teeth while White-Rabbit placed it in shackles.

I was gentler with the smaller RAT.

White-Rabbit was ruthless with the big RAT. She considered the RATs predators and rodents.

She dragged the big RAT over to a clock tower of rotting bricks. A white mist swirled around the base.

"What is this spooky place?"

"We can hide the RATs in the tower while you make a plan," White-Rabbit said. "The big RAT must first have new clothes. How embarrassing to be seen with a creature wearing torn pants."

A PRISONER ESCAPES

The little RAT tried to convince us that it was a good admin tool, which just happened to work remotely. "I help fix computers for a team with members located in different cities, which is why my pockets are filled with mouses."

The small RAT was running around the cell trying to catch the mouses that had jumped from its pockets.

No telling what White-Rabbit might do to the big RAT because it was now lying on the floor dirtying its clothes.

I yanked out a piece of cheese from my pocket and threw the cheese into the cell. "I'll make sure White-Rabbit doesn't hurt you, if you promise to help me," I whispered to the big RAT.

It spoke with a rough accent, like a sewer rat. "Anything you want, girlie. Just get me away from that creepy white bunny."

White-Rabbit's last comment before she went to sleep was, "Oh, dear, the big RAT has torn the sleeve of its new shirt. Whatever shall we do about the RAT?"

It was freaky the way White-Rabbit slept with her eyes wide open glaring at the big RAT. White-Rabbit would likely do away with the big RAT when she woke up because the RAT did not have good fashion sense.

I quietly lifted the key to the jail cell from the bunny's pocket. I pushed the sleeping White-Rabbit aside and entered the jail cell.

By the time White-Rabbit woke up, I was dangling the big Rat's shackles from my hand, and its wrists were free.

The door clanged shut.

I stood in a corner, surrounded by mouses and two RATs. "Come on, White-Rabbit, unlock the door," I yelled in a shaky voice.

She just stared with mean eyes.

"Okay. What do you want?" I said with a big sigh.

"If the Rats get you back to your world, you must turn me into a fashion model," she ordered.

I was really not into fashion video games. "I promise to find some fashion shows for avatars," I grumbled.

"Goodbye then!" Poof! The door opened and White-Rabbit vanished.

Quick, I grabbed the big RAT and jumped out of the cell with it.

I slammed the door on the smaller RAT and the mouses it controlled. "If you're a good RAT, then your team will restart you. At that point, you will vanish from this cell. Good luck to you," I said.

"Wait, you might need my help. Take me with you," the smaller RAT hollered.

"If you're a really a good RAT, then why did you enter the computer through a hole dug by a mole? A user would have invited you in to help," I said.

The little RAT appeared more cunning than the big RAT. Its beady eyes shifted as if it was searching for an excuse.

Well, two Remote Administration Tools might be better than one, so I freed the small RAT from the jail cell but kept it shackled like I had the big RAT.

A familiar, heart-wrenching whinny echoed from a cell near the exit of the tower. "I did not really mean to do it, Monsieur Enchanter, not really. I confess. Do not make me into a door nail!"

"Barebones?" I said and poked my face at the barred window.

The horsey, security guard looked out from between the bars. The prison bars framed a stick-horse, wearing the white collar of a priest. A long, white, Louis IV type wig framed its face. Spiral curls flowed from its skull to the middle of its pipe-like body. Barebones had tied a blue, French scarf around its nose holes and mouth. "Who goes there?" Its voice was muffled by the scarf, but still understandable.

"It's me. Jupiter!"

"How did you get inside the computer, mademoiselle? I do not remember; so much has happened. I am practicing my confession. The Enchanter accuses me of being a traitor. He has called for the same guillotine that beheaded the French king. There is to be a trial at four o'clock in the *City of Memory Chips*. I have put on my confessing collar. I am so sorry; I did not mean to do it," the horse said, wiping its eyes against the bars.

"Who or what exactly is the Enchanter?" I said, remembering that the brand name of the computer was *Enchanter*.

"The Enchanter is our CPU, our Central Processing Unit. The Enchanter is a wizard. Without him, we can do nothing."

"Does the Enchanter accuse you, because he thinks I hacked into the computer while you were in charge of security?"

"Ah, you must not worry your heart out, human. They believe lightning shorted out the computer, because the PC was not plugged into a surge protector."

"The computer was not plugged into anything," I mumbled.

"I am in prison, due to a Trojan-virus. Since I am the head of security, it is my fault the Trojan infected the computer and now threatens the lives of everyone even you, Jupiter."

"How did this Trojan-virus get in?" I asked.

Barebones explained that a Trojan horse carried the virus.

The Trojan horse had told me it had a virus, which I thought then was a common cold and not a deadly computer virus. "I'll help you escape from prison," I squeaked.

"Ah, mademoiselle, nobody has ever escaped from the Tower," the stick-horse said. Barebones pointed to a window in the hallway.

Alligator tails flopped across a water pool surrounding the tower.

"There are alligators in the moat?" I said.

"No, just their tails can be downloaded from the Chinese Internet. Alligators are fashion donors, who give their bodies to become laptop carry bags," Barebones said.

"I am so very sorry."

"Why are you sorry? It is the alligators' wish to be fashionable. Do not weep for the alligators. Their bags are dyed in many colors."

"I am extremely sorry for you, Barebones."

"Do not feel so guilty," the stick-horse said.

My mouth dropped open. "Then, you know that it was I who..."

"Yes, you let the Trojan-virus loose," Barebones said.

Barebones could not see the RATs standing by the door. The big RAT ground its teeth, a sign that it was happy at the news that I released the virus. Therefore, I said no more about being sorry.

The stick-horse cocked its skull in a curious manner. "Your eyes are watering, mademoiselle. I am programmed with little memory and a list of instructions, whereas you are still human with a heart and a brain."

"There is longing in your voice, Barebones."

"Impossible! Jupiter, be careful or the virus will strike you, too. Cover your face for protection against the virus." The stick-horse untied the scarf from its mouth and threw the scarf at me. "What happened to your teeth hardware?"

"I lost my braces," I said, picking up the scarf.

"Au revoir, until we meet again."

The stick-horse hopped away from the window.

The key to the RATs' cell worked on the lock of Barebone's prison cell, and I yanked open the door. "I can't let the Enchanter delete you, because of me. Come with us."

"Us?" Barebones said.

Both RATs stuck their heads into the cell.

"Eek! What are you doing here with RATs? I'd rather take my chances with the Enchanter," Barebones said.

"Don't be stupid," I said and pushed the stick-horse from the jail cell.

The big RAT snapped its teeth at Barebones and laughed at the shaking stick-horse.

"Some security," the small RAT snorted.

"No wonder you got a Trojan-virus into the computer, Boss," the big RAT said with deep admiration.

"Yeah," I said in a tough sounding voice. I needed the big RAT to think I was a criminal.

As soon as we left the tower, the stick-horse insisted on going its own way. "They'll be looking for me. I have no wish to endanger you, mademoiselle," Barebones said.

"My face is on a milk carton," I said.

The big RAT bowed. "My hero," it said and lowered its back so that I could ride it.

The stick-horse ran in one direction. I rode the RAT in the other direction. The small RAT led the way. There was no longer a need for shackles for either RAT. Both RATs pledged to obey me. I gained the big RAT's respect because it believed I was trying to destroy the computer. I had to go along and pretend to be a cracker who needed help from my brother, a pirate, in order to annihilate everything.

"Including us?" the big RAT said with a wide grin.

The big RAT was obviously crazy.

As for the small RAT, as soon as it discovered from Barebones that I was a user, it dropped the three mouses hidden in its pockets and swore allegiance to me.

Two RATs were now under my control. With any luck, the RATs could help me escape back to my world.

According to Barebones, the Trojan-virus could destroy everything in the computer, including me, a digital human girl.

B. Austin, Belinda Austin

HANGING OUT WITH A DVD DRIVE

The big RAT ran its programming code and took control of the computer camera. The Rat removed a bag tied to a cane. It then held the cane up, and I looked through the handle and was able to see the entire study.

The bedroom door lay on the carpet, its hinges dangling from the frame. There was no sign of my big brother Axel.

The north study wall was thumb tacked with his posters of vampires, monster trucks, and football schedules.

My posters of Math tables and greatest movie quotes hung on the south study wall.

On the ceiling were glow-in-the-dark stars and planets.

In the family picture hanging on the east wall, Dad seemed to snap his suspenders, his moustache vibrating with displeasure.

Mom's belly shook with shock, her hair standing on end.

Axel glared with different colored eyes making him look cross-eyed. Axel was born with a brown eye and a green eye. My brother was proud of his oddity and refused to wear contact lenses to correct his eye coloring.

Axel's thin face seemed to grow bigger in the family picture, while my eyebrow in the photo arched higher. Axel was six inches taller and muscular. He had hogged the camera that day. The photographer snapped only my left eye and brow.

Unfortunately, no one was in the study.

A crack of light shone above me.

"There's a way out! Take me to the top of the computer," I ordered the big RAT.

"Boss, a RAT is a better swimmer than climber," it said.

"Fine! I will go by myself. Turn on the speakers and the microphone. Both of you wait here."

The RATs nodded their heads.

I shoved the *Irresponsible Jupiter* file-folder between my teeth. I pulled myself up wires which hung like branches from the walls and inched toward the light and a metal ledge.

The ledge was slippery. I stretched my fingers to a slit from where the light shone, but the opening was too high.

Screws in the wall were as useful as a mountain climber's tools. Huffing and puffing, I heaved myself up to the next screw, climbing from one screw to the other, and another.

I hauled myself up to the last screw near where the light shone through.

I grabbed onto a higher ledge, lifting my leg up.

I peeked through the slit into the study.

I was on the DVD drive! A girl, narrower than a DVD, should be able to exit through this opening.

I began to squeeze my way through the slit.

Suddenly, a DVD popped in.

I pushed against the DVD. "Axel, do not put the DVD in the drive!" I shouted.

The big RAT had turned the microphone on because I heard my brother mutter, "The DVD is sticking in the drive. Darn computer is making that buzzing noise again."

The buzzing noise was I. The RAT had turned the speakers on, but Axel could not hear my words because I was tiny.

"Axel! It's Jupiter," I yelled with all my might.

Jeez, now my voice sounded like crackling electricity through the speakers.

The DVD clicked into place, spinning me on the disk.

Axel said, "Letters have been left on the screen." He read the message:

To whom it may concern—Help!
Computer gnomes kidnapped me.
It is not my fault.
I did not break the study window. Alicia

"What the heck does that mean?"

Eek! I mistakenly left a mirror message! Instead, I should have written the message backwards. The message written in red lipstick on the monitor screen had been understandable to me. For Axel, sitting *in front* of the monitor, the words would appear backwards to him. Axel would have to put a mirror up to the message to read the gibberish correctly.

"Screen needs to be refreshed," Axel said. "The gibberish is erased now. No harm done," he said. "Mm, Dad's email tool is open."

My heart beat excitedly, knowing Axel had no qualms about reading Dad's email.

"Darn, mail server is down," he said.

The DVD shook, rattling me on the disk.

The DVD whirled so fast, my head spun. As data bytes transferred from the DVD to the memory of the computer, I slid across the disk, my legs zipping like scissors.

I lost my balance and flew off the DVD.

Quick, I grabbed onto the edge of the DVD and hung on for dear life. My legs dangled in the air as the disk spun.

Far below, the big RAT lumbered away. The big RAT must have thought I was done for, and took off with its cane and thus, the ability to look through the camera to the study.

Hopefully, the big RAT turned the speakers back on and left the microphone on. If only I could communicate with Axel!

B. Austin, Belinda Austin

My fingernails were losing their grip on the DVD.

A PIRATE COMES TO MY RESCUE

I yelled down at the small RAT to, "Get me back on the DVD." In a millisecond, I was back on the DVD, spinning like a lightning-fast merry-go-round. With the RAT's help, I was stable. The spinning disk did not throw me off.

My only chance now of speaking to Axel was to play the DVD game with him.

With the aid of the small RAT, I became a player in the video game. There was a cool side effect of being a cast member of a video game DVD. While spinning dizzily on the disk, I also stood in a desert background of a video game. It was awesome being in two places at once, the DVD, and the monitor. My reflection was in the mirrored closet behind Axel. Once again, I looked scared yet I gripped a spinning disk, screaming with joy.

It was nerve-wracking that Axel pirated a new game named *The Wrath of the Gnome King*. The game was in *beta mode*, so not yet ready for public release. Axel was impatient so he stole a copy. Oops! I mean Axel pirated a copy. Axel claimed there was a difference since he never sold the merchandise but pirated from the Internet for his own use.

Dust blew about desert scenery, with eerie, howling noises. Barefoot gnomes with long noses littered the desert. The gnomes held knives, spoons, and other cutlery as weapons. They appeared frozen in place.

In the center of the game was a golden crown sticking out of the middle of a rusted boulder, from which volcanic magma flowed. In the far background were slim, black trees, which appeared as if a fire had rushed through the forest.

A pirate ship rocked on an ocean. The game had three terrains, all mixed together with three suns.

The game was not virtual reality so the volcano was not warm. Axel sat on the study chair, gawking at me standing on top of the rusted boulder. My brother was so flabbergasted; his green eye darkened and matched his brown eye better. His face flushed an angry red. "Jupiter, what are you doing playing my video game, *The Wrath of the Gnome King*? This is not a Multiuser Edition," he said, matter-of-factly. Then he mumbled, "What am I doing talking to an animated GIF?"

"I am not a GIF," I answered.

Axel leaned back in the armless chair, with his arms folded across his chest. An amused look was on his face, as if it was commonplace to be in two places at once.

Well, being in two places at once was new to me. I sweated from three suns, which made me feel as if I was melting. My face was green from spinning on the disk, and my stomach retched. Moreover, I feared Axel could still not hear me. "Help! I really am inside the computer! This is no game, Axel!"

His face grew bigger as he thrust his head at the monitor screen. "The GIF has my bratty sister's attitude," he grumbled.

"It's because this is really me. I've become a digital girl, Axel."

"Well, you are in such big trouble, for cracking the monitor," he said, laughing and clearly not believing me.

"It's just a hairline crack; the bump on my head is bigger. You should be in trouble for pirating this video game, plus the music you're playing, which I know you didn't pay for."

"I only download copyrighted stuff for myself. I don't distribute," he muttered, frowning. There was doubt in his eyes now that perhaps I was telling the truth about being inside the computer.

"You're still a thieving pirate." I pointed to a copy of *Pirate Magazine,* which lay on his lap. His black t-shirt had an iron-on picture of a green-faced monitor, wearing an eye patch, and a pirate hat with a skull and bones insignia. A wooden leg with a hook was shoved through the picture of the monitor. It looked as if the hook was the left ear, and the wooden peg the right ear. Printed on the t-shirt was his tattooed avatar — Bulldog.

Axel rubbed his chest, running his hand down the computer pirate emblem on his shirt. He cleared his throat. "Well, since you're the infamous White-Rabbit, we've both joined the dark side of computing."

"I'm a hacker who breaks into computers, and does not burglarize them. I follow the ethics of the Nerds Computing Club. I simply like the challenge."

"Well, we still work in stealth and play a role in the computer underground. Look how you hacked into my video game."

"Computer-gnomes shrunk me and kidnapped me," I said.

Axel turned pale as a ghost. "Wait one minute! You are an avatar in my video game and you are talking to me like a person? What happened to the chair-arms?" he said suspiciously.

"Well, one is on the study floor, as you well know." I picked up the shrunken chair-arm that was on the floor of the monitor and held the chair-arm up to him. "I tried to hold onto the chair, but the gnomes got me. The gnomes used my shoestring to haul me to the camera after shrinking me with their magic." I lifted my shoe that was missing a shoestring.

He mumbled, "There was a shoestring hanging from the monitor." He grabbed the mouse and started clicking and sliding it across the mouse pad. "I wondered how you simply vanished. The window is broken. I figured you got scared when I broke down the door."

"Why would I jump two stories out the window?"

"Because you're stupid. Jupiter! What did you do with the mouse? It doesn't work!"

"Dormouse hacked in and erased the mouse driver."

Axel clicked on the keyboard using the arrow keys. He tried multiple combinations to download a new mouse driver, access the computer register keys, execute system files, etc. He tried to bring up the Trash folder to search for the deleted mouse driver. He plugged in another mouse. Nothing worked. Everything was still frozen, except for me.

Axel frantically flipped through a game manual, throwing it on the floor in disgust. He grabbed the monitor sides and yelled, "Jupiter, I just installed this game. I transferred the game files to the hard disk earlier. The game advertised magical bonus features, on invisible DVD tracks. I thought this sounded cool, but the gnomes have taken control of the computer."

"Well, you're the gamer. Do something!"

"I have no experience with this game. I don't even know the rules."

Even though Axel had not clicked the game *Start* button, the gnomes began to thaw from their locked positions, sounding like cracking ice.

I screamed, ducking my head, as stalagmites and stalactites hurled at me like swords.

Axel had only added two pirates to his crew so far and his own bulldog avatar.

Odd, Axel's voice echoed from behind, saying these words, "Hey, kid sister!"

The doppelganger-side-effect of video games, which can infect a player, was a rare phenomenon. Axel's miniature double, his tiny doppelganger, was inside the computer, waving from behind. He jumped up and down by the wires and monitor guts, while at the same time, the human Axel sat in the study, in the real world. However, Axel's doppelganger was not his mere reflection, nor was Axle controlling him. The doppelganger had a brain. The pint-sized Axel danced inside the monitor, whistling and singing, happy to have materialized. The only other difference between the two Axels was their switched eyes. The real Axel had a right green eye and a left brown eye. His mirror image, the cyber Axel, had a right brown eye and a left green eye.

"This is not good," Axel said in the study and mumbled, "There is a digital version of myself in the computer, an independent game player with a will of its own. This is a first in video games and untested since it comes from gnomes. I should never have taken that game, the only copy available for anyone to download, almost as if it was meant just for me. I'm really sorry, Jupiter, that this pirated game infected the PC with the gnomes who kidnapped you. I planned to erase the download after I copied it to the DVD so Dad wouldn't find it, but then you took over the study."

Axel pushed the DVD eject button.

The magic DVD he had copied from the download would not eject.

B. Austin, Belinda Austin

THE WRATH OF THE GNOME KING

Gnomes gnashed their teeth. One gnome carried a net to capture me. Axel's pirate avatar, Bulldog, and the other two pirates bravely fought the gnomes off.

The avatar, Bulldog, resembled a man with the head of a bulldog. He had tattooed arms and wore a striped shirt and sweater cap, like a sailor. He smoked a pipe. Bulldog growled and bit the gnomes. Unfortunately, Axel had not yet chosen a weapon for his avatar when the gnomes attacked. Bulldog and the pirates were soon outnumbered.

The pirates vanished from the game, leaving behind a sword and flag with skull and crossbones.

"The game is buggy," Axel said and sounded frustrated.

Gnomes chased me. "Do you think the game is buggy, Sherlock?" I yelled at Axel. "What with a giant bug walking around like it owns the game!" I circled the volcano.

"Come back here! Don't you get smart with me," Axel said.

I came back around the volcano. "Well one of us has to be smart! You're so dumb playing a pirated game filled with gnomes," I shouted.

"Well I'm not the idiot trapped inside the computer," he yelled back. "Oh, blasted! Here they come! If only I could man the pirate ship."

The abandoned ship rocked on an oasis in the middle of a desert. A large palm tree growing from sand shaded the ship.

"It's the bug that has the game confused," I said.

Axel's mini-double sweated. He was dressed for warmth with a high-necked shirt and jacket. My brother's doppelganger clearly did not wish to fight. He stood on the pirate ship with his hands on his hips. Axel's double began a long, lengthy speech about making peace.

"Too bad your doppelganger is not courageous," I said to Axel.

A gnome hit me on the head with a giant ladle. The gnome looked like my grandma, but I punched his nose anyway.

Mini-Axel, the doppelganger, was definitely my brother. "I'll help you, Jupiter," the mini said reluctantly.

He grabbed a rope, hanging from the pirate ship. Mini-Axel swung to the boulder.

He steadied his rocky feet, before letting the rope go, and he yanked the sword from the stone, raising it in victory.

The digital Axel stood with his knees bent, and his sword pointed at the gnomes. I had never been so proud of my brother, even if he was just his doppelganger.

He whirled the sword around, knocking off some gnomes' heads.

The other gnomes ran towards mini-Axel. They climbed the boulder, slipping, sliding, and snarling.

Gnomes stood on each other's shoulders, forming a ladder to the top of the rock.

I hid behind a cactus.

There was a sound of trumpets, followed by dancing fairies. The Gnome King marched in front of the procession. The Gnome King was the tallest of the gnomes. The king was, also, the ugliest. He had a big, crooked nose, long pointy ears, and teeth like a picket fence. His big ears kept a large crown from falling off his head.

A brown bug crawled in front of the king. The bug was so enormous its antennae looked more like horns.

The bug pointed its antennae at Axel's doppelganger.

Gnomes captured mini-Axel and dragged him before the king.

The Gnome King pointed a long finger at the doppelganger, demanding to know, "Where is your sister?"

Given that the doppelganger tried to reach me and risked his own freedom, I now thought of him as I would my brother. *I must free Axel*, I thought.

It was as if my other brother, the Axel sitting in the study all safe and sound, could hear my thoughts. He shook his head and mouthed the words, *you better not, Jupiter.* He pointed at a hag dressed in white, walking towards the king and his ragtag court of gnomes and worshipful fairies.

It was the W–W–W, the infamous Wicked-Witch-West! The witch was short and mean looking. She had buggy eyes and a long sharp nose that grew from the top of her forehead. She was dressed in rags that swept her feet. The witch had bad teeth. She was the avatar of one of the greediest persons ever.

The witch had her own followers, some of the Oz hackers. The hackers looked in terrible shape. She had clearly taken her fury out on them because their hacking skills were not good enough to find the pot of gold at the end of the rainbow.

"Jupiter is the latest technology and no one had claimed the digital human," the witch said.

My heart beat fearfully. *What did the witch mean that no one had claimed me? Had, like in past tense!*

With her huge nostrils, the witch had a nose for money. She sniffed a piece of paper and sighed with rapture. "I have just come from the Internet and the United States Patent and Trademark office," she said, waving the paper. "I have registered a patent on Jupiter. The technology of digital humans now belongs to me. Jupiter is more valuable than a pot of gold at the end of the rainbow."

My knees shook at the thought of being enslaved to the Wicked-Witch-West like the Oz hackers. The witch had beat up Tin-Man for not finding a pot of gold. The Tin-Man now resembled a crushed tin can, walking around with big feet.

She had beheaded Scarecrow and just a stick stuck up from his collar. Now, she claimed to own me because she filed a piece of paper with the U.S. Patent office on my technology.

"Surrender your sister," the witch said to Axel. "I must take Jupiter apart and see how she works."

I was so scared at the thought of being dissected, that I fell off the spinning DVD.

I FALL DOWN A
COMPUTER HOLE

I screamed, falling down a dark hole. "Jupiter!" the two Axels hollered, followed by eerie silence.

Clouds crammed with pictures and thoughts resembling comic strips, whizzed by. I must have fallen into the computer's memory banks.

Suddenly, a light flashed. There was a whirling noise, and a rug shot out of a circuit board.

The flying carpet kept trying to get under me.

I struggled to stay away from the rug, thinking that it belonged to the witch. There was also the fact that we had been playing the buggy, video game *Wrath of the Gnome King* in a desert. Advanced-desert transport was not to be trusted. This mode of transportation is rare. Nowadays, flying carpets are found only at *The Museum of Carpets and World of Flying Carpets* display.

Memory chips were below with sharp pins sticking up that looked painful to fall on them. There was no choice but to swing my legs onto the flying carpet, to avoid falling into a pit of thorny hardware.

In a déjà vu moment, I flew through the Java party's flowered archway.

The flying carpet landed on what was left of the picnic table.

The carpet flipped, depositing me on a serving plate. Ouch! My ankle was twisted.

The carpet stuffed an apple in my mouth and then wrapped my nose and mouth with the scarf Barebones had given me. The carpet tied me up like a trussed turkey. It then transformed into a checkered tablecloth, sliding beneath me.

A dinner bell went ting-a-ling.

Okay, now I was in for it. The witch planned to carve me up like a turkey in order to inspect my technology. I could not scream for help, due to the apple in my mouth. Anyway, my only companion was Oxy-Moron. His flat head lay on the ground. "The silence is deafening. Thank you for calling and have a nice day," Oxy-Moron said in his Indian accent.

I bit into the apple, planning to eat my way through the scarf and out of my current danger.

A small, jeweled crown and bare foot stuck out from the side of a Java cup. A hoe and spade leaned against the cup, along with a treasure bag pile.

"The Gnome King," I mumbled with a mouth full of apple bits. The king cleverly disguised himself as a garden gnome, perhaps to fool the witch.

He stepped from his hiding place. The king untied me and removed the apple from my mouth.

"Thanks, your Majesty," I said and quickly rewrapped the scarf around my face for protection against the virus that had attacked the Java party. Green slime was everywhere so I tightened the scarf. Since I was flat, like a paper doll, the sides of my head touched, giving me a wallop of a headache.

The king was pleased that I recognized him.

"It's because you are uglier than the other gnomes," I said, without thinking.

He stood with his fists on his hips, thanking me for gloriously insulting him, as only a ruler should be. He snapped his fingers, transforming his garden rags into royal blue, fur-lined clothes. Gnomes tended to be antisocial and rarely spoke, even to each other, yet here was the King of Gnomes, smiling while he puffed on a backward-S pipe. Suddenly, he lifted a scepter above my head, as if he would stab my throat. "I have been watching you, user, for some time," he said with a thick, German accent. "As Gnome King, I cannot take credit for something we did not do. It was you, Jupiter, who broke into the computer, not us. You must take credit for this, accept awards, make speeches, and all other honor that comes when you have done a good job. You must not give credit for your escapades to the White-Rabbit, but should use your real name."

I said, "And you should admit to being stupid. You cannot even spell. The email you sent read, *We no who u r. We have been watching u.*"

"I don't need a spell checker to spell *delete forever*. The Enchanter will ensure you are forever erased and cannot be recycled from the trash. I shall turn you in and claim the reward of becoming a desktop icon. You are sweating, Cracker, and you are trembling," he said.

"I am not a cracker. You know, darn well, your gnomes kidnapped me!"

He licked his finger, running his digit down my cheek, and then stuck the finger in his mouth. "You taste salty, which proves you are a cracker."

"Tears are salty, stupid!" I shivered from the saliva he left on my skin.

"Do not be upset. The Enchanter would not delete a bunny, or a cracker," he said.

"Why, then, is the Enchanter after me?"

"The Enchanter put your name on a milk carton because you were last seen with the Trojan horse. In the horse's belly was the virus that is infecting the computer's health. The 21st

Century is the dawn of the healthy computer. Energy-saving CPUs even do yoga now. When you think the computer is running slow, or stuck, and you click and bang-bang your mouse, it is the Enchanter, meditating, floating above memory chips with his knees open, and sitting in his yoga pose."

"I won't take credit for the Trojan-virus. Your Trojan-gnomes directed the fleas," I said.

"It is a computer-gnome's nature to direct chaos."

The king took a bite out of a sheet of paper that looked awful familiar. "That's my..." I said.

"Yes, your English essays taste scrumptious, Jupiter, especially all the white lies and tall tales."

"I apologize for blaming you for eating my homework," I blurted out.

"Too late for sorry," the King said.

There had been a Java party earlier, but there was no one here now except for the Gnome King, Cuckoo, and me. The spelling bee hung passed out over an empty Java cup. Its wing drooped over the cup.

Suddenly, the bee's stinger stuck straight up in the air, and then pointed to the corner.

The king walked over to the *Java Virtual Machine*. He flipped up the nozzle, and slid beneath the machine with his mouth wide open. No drops of Java fell on his tongue. He shoved his fist through the empty machine.

Eureka! Cuckoo was trying to tell me that Java programmed a game as magical as the Wrath of the Gnome King. This means the king must have more Java to increase his supernatural powers.

I earlier hid a pot full of Java under the table. I now inched my way to the foot of the table where the Java was hidden.

I shoved the pot under the king's nose. "Would you like a cup, your Majesty," I said with a sweet smile.

He held an empty cup, the cup rattling against the saucer. "Kind acts do not change things between us, digital human. You are too valuable. I must turn you in for the reward so my desktop icon will be forever undeletable. I shall become more powerful and at last, overthrow the Enchanter. I will become Emperor of this computer," he said.

I threw the Java pot at his face, and the king dropped to his knees.

I hobbled toward the flowered archway.

The king sucked the Java from his royal robe. He then swept the ground with his tongue.

"Where's my army? Go after her, numbskulls! Do I have to do everything myself?" the king yelled. "March! March!"

Gnomes popped up from nowhere, littering the garden. They danced in lines, fluttering their legs like Irish stepdancers.

A helicopter buzzed overhead.

A chair popped down from a rope hanging from the helicopter.

Axel's doppelganger grinned down at me. He wore sunglasses and a pilot's uniform.

I sat on the chair, and he lifted me into the chopper.

I hugged my brother's doppelganger. My arms went right through his body.

"I'm unstable," Axel said. He waved about as if a shotgun blasted him. He let off electrical sparks.

"Oh, Axel, you don't look well," I said.

He was bald and his nose smashed into his face, which was a grayish color. His brown eye was missing.

"I barely survived playing level 1. This is level 2," he said, groaning.

"What can I do to help?" I said, panicking.

"I'm low on memory," he said.

Axel concentrated on flying the helicopter through a cyber forest of rainbow-colored trees.

His head hit the bubble windshield, with a loud crack.

The helicopter spun, crashing into the woods.

B. Austin, Belinda Austin

EVER BEEN BURNED
INTO A SCREEN?

I limped from the burning helicopter while pulling Axel from the wreckage. What was left of my brother's doppelganger was a mess of wires. Nevertheless, I counted, "One, two. Come on, Axel! Restart the game! Please! You've got to advance to level 3."

He fluttered his eyelashes, pulling weakly at my hand. "I came to warn you," he whispered. He shifted his eyes to the right, his body stiffening.

I turned my head to what he was looking at, expecting gnomes to litter the forest, but instead...

"Quick! Look away!" Axel said.

"It's me. I've been cloned," I whispered. "How did I duplicate?"

"The pirated game was magical and buggy," he gasped. It took most of Axel's strength to speak. "Never stare at the other Jupiter's eyes. To lock eyes with your own doppelganger is a death omen."

"No, Axel, the other Jupiter is just bad luck, like you are. To see a relative's doppelganger is a sign of danger or bad luck," I said, hastily. Yet, having my doppelganger, looking over my shoulder and breathing into my ear, creeped me out.

"I can't hold on much longer. I'm sorry to have let you down, little sister," Axel said in a weak voice.

"Oh, Axel, you never let me down. You saved me from the Gnome King. I did not mean it about bad luck. You're my brother, my good luck charm." I tried to grasp his hand, but my hand went right through his. "Stay with me! Axel, please! Don't leave me!"

He shivered and an odd sensation tingled up my arm. The sparks he let off were like glowing cinders. Axel felt like ashes yet, I could still feel the grass beneath his ghostly hand.

Slowly...Axel faded.

"No!" It was as if I was drowning. "Axel, no! Axel!"

"Jupiter, I'm still here."

"Axel?" His voice came from behind.

Axel was trapped inside a block of ice. He let out a deep sigh and then a devastating silence. He had become screen burn-in. When a non-moving image is left in place for too long on a monitor, the image might be burned into the monitor screen, which is why screen savers were invented. The image would resemble a ghost of the original.

That darn buggy video game! I pounded the ice, pushing and shoving from the outside, but could not cause even a crack in the cube.

My own doppelganger had vanished.

I fell back and laid flat on the grass. I cried myself to sleep.

GHOSTS AND DOPPELGANGERS

The slightest wisp of movement woke me. "Axel?" I said, turning my head toward the large ice cube. The ice had melted. My brother's doppelganger was gone. My own doppelganger was lying down and hugging me.

I screamed and twisted my head to avoid my doppelganger's eyes. Quick, I snatched my file from the ground and ran.

Branches scratched my arms, yet I stumbled deeper into the woods.

Someone breathed heavily.

I breathed out.

Someone breathed in.

Branches reached out.

I screamed, moving faster.

Something brushed against my cheek.

I waved my arms, but nothing was there.

Someone or something pushed against my back.

I limped toward a spot of light, shaped like a teardrop.

I stopped and hugged my hands to my aching sides.

A swarm of ghostly images flew past.

I flung my arms out and covered my head.

"Jupiter," a muffled voice said.

I felt goose bumps on my arms. "Show yourself then and quit acting so scary. Do not be offended when I don't look at you," I said, thinking it must be my doppelganger.

My stalker stepped out from behind a tree and held up his palms. "It's me. Axel," he said and sounded as if he was speaking with cotton in his mouth.

"Oh, Axel, I'm so happy to see you," I said, shivering with fear. Once again, my brother's doppelganger transformed into something else. "However did you escape?"

"I graduated to level 3 in the video game."

My wonderful brother was still trying to save me. Axel was still working in the study wracking his brain on a plan of rescue.

"But I can see right through you," I said.

"I know," he said with a deep sigh. "I've turned into a ghost."

He is no longer Axel's doppelganger but his ghost image, I thought. Ghosting is normally done to create a clone for backup and restore purposes.

"Something is very wrong with the computer, Jupiter. I have tried everything to stop the video game and restart. The computer is running without electricity. Even weirder, the battery power backup, the UPS, is dead."

"You pirated a game containing gnome magic, so I'm not surprised."

"With my upgraded game level, I should have reverted back to my doppelganger self but instead, I'm even more unstable."

"You are Axel's ghost image and therefore, a clone of my brother."

"I'm a ghost."

"You should not be unstable."

"I'm actually a fragment, left behind by level 2. Consequently, I may vanish at any moment. Thinking about my unstableness makes me jittery." He wiggled about like snow on a television screen.

"Your condition might be caused by the virus," I said.

"My computer has a virus?"

"You mean *our* computer has a virus."

"Jupiter! You didn't!"

"Of course not," I said, crossing my fingers behind my back.

"Why is the Gnome King after you then?" he said suspiciously.

"No reason," I squeaked.

"Jupiter," he said in his big brother, scolding tone.

I stamped my foot. "Oh, alright, the Gnome King tricked me and I let in a virus. I did not do anything wrong."

"Right! So, this mess is *not* your fault," he said, giving me a familiar look.

The darkening sky caused my knees to knock together. "We must find a way out," I said, changing the subject. I flung away the folder labeled *Irresponsible Jupiter*.

"What was that you just threw?" he said.

"Nothing, just a lesson learned."

"According to the game manual, an opening is this way," he said.

If Axel's doppelganger was unstable, maybe he was not trustworthy. "You think an opening is this way? You don't know for sure?" I said.

Suddenly, something shoved my shoulder, pushing me to my knees.

My doppelganger ran away, laughing wickedly.

Axel held out a hand to help me rise.

I grabbed at his ghostly hand, shivering at a cold, fog sensation. My hand went right through him. I bit my lip, holding back my tears.

"Jupiter, I know you're a good person and mean well. This time, it really is not your fault that your doppelganger is black-hearted, like an evil twin," he said.

I wailed because everything went dark. "Axel?"

"Your brother...I, must be rebooting the computer."

"Maybe the computer is dying from the virus. I'm sorry."

The lights went on and Axel smiled. "You're growing up, Jupiter. Your last thoughts are of me and not of yourself."

"Growing up hurts too much," I mumbled.

Presto! At these words, a childhood friend hopped in front of us. My old avatar, March-Hare, blocked our way. "I've waited for you two years, Jupiter," she said.

B. Austin, Belinda Austin

MAD AS A MARCH HARE

I was born a natural technology whiz. I began my hacking career at the age of eight on a cold spring day in March. The avatar I chose for my handle then was March-Hare.

The bunny wore large gold-rimmed glasses and a big yellow tie with orange polka dots tied around its neck. It blinked its big eyes at me.

"I've missed you," I said to March-Hare and bent to kiss the bunny's nose.

March-Hare moved her head, poking me in the eye with a long ear. Like most hares, March-Hare was shy.

"This is my brother," I said.

"I remember Axel," March-Hare grumbled. "I see you've turned another member of your family into a ghost."

"I've never turned anyone into a ghost. It's not my fault that Axel is a ghostly figure."

"Nothing is ever your fault, Jupiter. Since you abandoned your childhood, I would have thought by now you would be mature," March-Hare said.

"I have grown up," I said.

March-Hare made a face.

"Do you know the way out?" I said.

She hopped around and wiggled her tail. "I'll help lead you out."

"Come on, Axel," I said excitedly.

"March-Hare doesn't seem to like me," my brother said.

"March-Hare was always jealous. We didn't part on good terms."

"Well, what's going to happen to me when you leave?" Axel said.

"Is it cool being a ghost?"

"I guess I could pirate the internet more easily."

I rolled my eyes. Pirating was all Axel ever thought about, even his doppelganger.

We followed March-Hare out of the forest and into a clearing.

March-Hare hopped around. "Here we are!"

I turned in a circle. "We're still in the guts of the computer. There is no door or any way out."

"You never said you wanted to get out of the computer. I assumed you referred to the forest. You should say what you mean," March-Hare said.

"Well, I mean what I say, which is the same thing."

"Then you might as well say you want the computer to get out of you," March-Hare said.

"Oh, you're confusing!"

"Here. Drink some wine." March-Hare handed me an empty glass.

I held the glass out and waited. "Where is the wine?"

"There isn't any wine," March-Hare said.

"Then it wasn't very civil of you to offer wine," I said angrily.

"Then it wasn't very civil of you to abandon me when you left elementary school." March-Hare boxed my nose.

"You're mad," I said.

"I am furiously heartless," March-Hare said, hopping continuously.

"I meant that you're crazy."

"I meant that you broke my heart, Jupiter. After three years together, you deserted me on Easter before enrolling in Middle School!"

"I grew up and needed an avatar who reflected more of who I had become."

"You mean not a fat, short bunny!"

"You mean cute baby fat," I said.

"A ton of lard," March-Hare said.

"A ton is 2,000 pounds. You don't weigh a ton."

"I only eat carrots but still gain weight. It took a year to feel better about myself after you left."

"I'm happy for you, March-Hare. You don't seem as neurotic."

"I turned to the church and found religion, like the Easter Hare," she said.

"You mean, the Easter Bunny."

"There you go again, making me feel bad because I'm not a rabbit but a hare. Just when I was beginning to feel good about myself again, you rain on my Easter parade."

March-Hare picked her glasses up and straightened her tie. She cleared her throat and recited: "When I was a child, I used to speak like a child, think like a child, reason like a child; when I became a middle-school hacker, I did away with childish things, such as my bunny."

"That's sort of from the Bible," I said.

"The verse is from the book of Corinthians, Chapter 13, verse 11. A copy of the Bible is in the archives. The Enchanter freed me from the archives where you dumped me. I am saved, Jupiter. Can you say the same about yourself, if the virus destroys this computer?"

March-Hare yanked from beneath the folds of her stomach a large red candy heart. The heart had the name Jupiter written in grey with a big black **X** over the name. March-Hare broke the candy heart in half and hopped away.

"Wait," I yelled. "Why did the Enchanter free you? What did you give him in return?"

"The Enchanter rewarded me with my own desktop icon," she shouted.

"You Judas," I yelled at March-Hare's back. She had turned me in.

A gang was coming towards us, and they did not look friendly.

HIS MOST MAGICAL ENCHANTER

Members of Brute Force Blocking Software surrounded the other Axel and me. Grim Reaper grabbed me around the waist. "The Enchanter demands to see you," she mumbled.

"I won't leave you," Axel said.

The virus had struck *Cyber City*. Green-slime covered about a third of the city. Neon lights wiggled on broken pavement, cloaking the city in semi-darkness. Hardware lay crushed beneath fallen windows. Most of the bright lights were out, and the fan no longer blew a warm breeze. Thus, frost engulfed the windows that were undamaged. Icicles hung from the window frames.

Human-like creatures burned software piles and huddled around the flames, trying to keep warm.

Shadowy figures stood in the fires' fringes, waving their arms about to fan the heat, like mock turtles swimming in the sea. Most of the cyber shadows were too weak to be threatening and sighed in melancholy voices.

"If the anti-virus was useless against the Trojan virus, even we could get infected, like these shadows," Axel said, gulping.

"Perhaps humans and ghosts are immune to the virus," I said.

Grim Reaper pinched my shoulder and glared.

"Maybe my brother and I are infected," I said loudly.

Grim Reaper ignored us.

My stomach was queasy. Perhaps it was the virus.

"I...your human brother, may be able to manually remove the virus, but he must first discover that the computer is infected," Axel whispered.

"But as his doppelganger, you are Axel, though he sits in the study playing *The Wrath of the Gnome King* or whatever. Can you tell my brother about the virus?" I whispered back.

"We have our own minds, though we share old memories. His order was to steal the helicopter. Once the helicopter was shot down, Axel no longer has a clue about my thoughts or actions."

"Thank goodness, a Trojan virus does not make copies of itself, like some viruses so it spreads slower. By now, maybe Axel has figured out that the computer has a virus," I said.

"A Trojan virus has the power to delete," he said, his voice sounding bleak. "Sometimes, the easiest solution to fix a Trojan is to erase everything and reinstall."

"Oh," I said, feeling faint. Surely Axel would realize that he would be erasing me.

"If a backup of the computer had been made after you were kidnapped by the gnomes, you could be restored from the backup," he said.

"I doubt there is a backup of the computer that recent. Axel will permanently erase me if he reinstalls," I said. "You might return when Axel plays a video game again, but I..."

Grim Reaper ripped off my scarf and snarled. "The virus deletes programs. Data vanishes. Programs crash into buildings and woodlands. Just look at what's happened to the city!"

"It was the beasties!" I yelled.

Axel shouted. "Protect my sister from the virus. Give her back the scarf."

"Jupiter does not need protection, since she is human," Grim Reaper said. Grim Reaper did not talk; she screeched, sounding like fingernails scraping a chalkboard.

"Don't believe her," Axel whispered. "The virus was created by a human, so you may catch it. Your race is creative, but also destructive. Maybe a portal of escape is nearby."

"If we could just get away from Grim Reaper," I said, sighing.

A flashing sign floated above the golden doors to the *Arena of Memory Chips*. The sign read, *Entertainment Today. Escape Feats, Card Games, Hat Tricks, Memory Pranks, Money Cons, Illusions, Supernaturals, and Executions. All conjured up by the Enchanter. All magic performed before a live audience, with no added visual effects.*

Grim Reaper shoved me through the door, and it closed behind us with a bang.

The circular arena was made of smoke and mirrors. In the center was a giant computer chip with sizzling circuits.

"That must be the Enchanter," Axel said. He pointed to a man-like creature dangling from the air above a computer chip. The Enchanter was the brains of the computer. The giant, grey computer chip stretched so high, it appeared bottomless at the other end.

The Enchanter was dressed like a wizard, except for a straitjacket he wore like a crazy man. The straitjacket bound the Enchanter's arms with the sleeves buckled to his back. A chain bound his ankle, wrapped around his chest, and then locked at the middle of his back.

The Enchanter hung upside down, so it was a wonder that

a purple top hat balanced on his head.

The Enchanter emitted electrical streaks from his veins and his skin stunk of burning wires. Smoke rings rose from his head. His clothes gave an occasional zap because the threads were electronic. He had a long, pointy-head, shaped like a volcanic brain.

Chairs floated in the air.

I chased a chair and caught one.

Axel, being a ghost, hung in the air.

It was eerily silent while the Enchanter swung in the air.

"What's he doing?" I whispered.

Popcorn kernels flew from every direction.

"Shush, he's solving the virus," a cyber-being said.

Hocus-pocus! A desk floated from the very air. A notebook was on the desk and a pen.

The Enchanter closed his eyes and dictated to the light pen. "Trojan-proxy relay-server. Crash. %*#$+.@. Reboot. Punching-card bag. Update ready for upload. Bad file descriptor. Fetch file. Filling Workstation. Operation now in progress. System reload. Ching, ching, ping, piggy bank, oink. File backup. The mind the question and arrows of time. The calamity of so long a life."

I jumped from the seat and leaped onto the stage. I grabbed his swinging head, slapping my hand over his mouth. "Speak English! I don't know the meaning of half that gibberish and I don't believe you do either!"

Everyone gasped.

The Enchanter had put my face on a milk carton, but there was no recognition in his eyes. He must be running low on memory due to the virus infecting him.

Quick, I ran back to the chair.

"Abracadabra," the Enchanter said in a bored voice. The chains fell and the straitjacket unraveled. The Enchanter landed on his feet, bowing to the audience, who gave him a standing ovation.

One cyber-being clapped his hands too slowly, and the Enchanter vaporized him with a zap of his fingers.

"I suppose you want a hat trick." The Enchanter pulled his top hat from his head. He circled a wand around the inside, displaying its empty contents.

The Enchanter yanked March-Hare from his hat, holding the hare by her long, floppy ears.

March-Hare was still mad and had obviously been in a fight. One front tooth was broken and her eye blackened. The bunny wore boxing gloves and kept trying to swing at me.

The Enchanter pulled a measuring tape from his top hat, measuring March-Hare. "You are as short as May, but longer than February. A jacket will do," he said, snapping his fingers.

He transformed the mad March-Hare into a furry straitjacket. The Enchanter dropped March-Hare back in his hat, which he then placed snugly on his head. The hat jiggled, the hare trying to escape the straitjacket.

The Enchanter waved his hand, vanishing in a puff of smoke.

He reappeared on a giant, super-chip, suspended above the audience. The Enchanter had changed to wizard's robes. His light pen was now a wand, which he zapped across the audience, turning a few of the cyber-beings into wormy apples.

The Enchanter held up the wand, and the crowd gasped. "Am I not your Central Processing Unit? I *am* the CPU. I *am* the computer and order thousands of instructions a second. With a blink, I am here. I am there. I am everywhere. Yet, I cannot find the Gnome King. The little twerp invited a virus in. Where is the Gnome King?" he thundered.

All the cyber-beings quaked in their seats.

The Enchanter squeezed his fists, screaming, "I am going to start executing each of you, until someone squeals. Off with your heads! You, the disk doctor." He pointed the wand to a man in a white suit, carrying a doctor's bag.

The man froze, his eyeballs spinning like two disks.

Grim Reaper swept the doctor up in her long arms. She threw the screeching doctor into a spinning pit surrounded by red bricks. Everyone cringed at his screams.

"I'm coming through. Make way or I'll burn you," a booming voice roared.

The crowd parted in the center.

A fire-breathing dragon flapped its wings.

"It's the Garbage-Collector," said a hushed voice, one of the cyber-beings. "The Collector burns up all the used memory, and recycles the ashes. Thank goodness, he has shown up to distract the Enchanter; otherwise, our CPU might delete us all. The virus has made the Enchanter insane. It is lunacy to delete the disk doctor during a plague. If the disks break, the computer will not work."

The crowd gasped.

"The Collector is pale and is, also, infected," the cyber-being murmured.

"What have you for us, Draggy," the Enchanter said, stroking the dragon's cheek.

"I know who the villain is who let in the virus to destroy this computer. The virus was carried in the belly of a Trojan horse."

I pulled my scarf up to the top of my head.

A BROTHER FOR A BROTHER

The crowd cheered at the dragon called the Collector. My doppelganger suddenly appeared, pushing me from the chair. "She is with the Gnome King," the other Jupiter sang.

The Collector grabbed my shoulders and dragged me to the Enchanter.

The Enchanter formed his eyebrows like thunderbolts, causing an explosion.

A guillotine fell on the stage, the sharp blade coming down with a bang.

The Enchanter zapped me.

I landed at the Enchanter's feet in an ungraceful heap. The mirrored surface was slippery.

A cyber-being pointed at me. "The creature isn't an avatar," it said.

"Yet, it looks like a flat avatar," another cyber-being agreed, "And it is digital." The cyber-being who said this had its nose in the air, like a know-it-all.

The two carried on a conversation, uncaring that I could hear them.

"The creature appears more like a photograph."

"A GIF file, perhaps?"

"You mean, a picture come to life, like an animated GIF?"

"Yes, that's it. The creature is flat and two-dimensional, like a moving picture, an animated GIF."

The Enchanter walked with his hands grasped behind his back. "You are a malicious user," he hissed at me.

"It's a user!"

All the cyber-beings chattered, pointing at me.

"A user has never been inside the *Arena of Memory Chips* before," the cyber-being who first began gossiping about me said. "The user has legs!"

They all stood on their seats, peering at me.

"The user's brain is weak, though," it noted.

"We had no idea that users are digital beings!"

A know-it-all cyber-being, who seemed smarter than the others, asked, "But aren't most users in 3-D?"

The Enchanter tugged my hair so I had to roll my eyes up to look at him. "Explain," he ordered.

"I had an accident and fell off a Trojan horse. I did not know he swallowed a computer virus. The virus is just a bunch of fleas, eating everything in their path. Don't you have flea spray?" I said.

The Enchanter turned all shades of red. "Does this look like a pet store, idiot? No shopping mall is here. This is not the Internet. I'm surprised a dumb user like you is the virus leader."

The Enchanter pointed the wand at me.

I fell to my knees, covering my face with my hands.

"I suppose you must have a proper trial." The Enchanter motioned to a server. "Download trial software from the Internet."

A desk emerged and landed in front of the Enchanter. A judge's gavel loomed in his hand.

Ten judges marched across the super-chip. They sat behind the Enchanter with dirty, bare feet, showing beneath their robes. They wore wigs like English judges.

"We must hurry. The Trial Software expires in five minutes, because justice was never really purchased," the Enchanter said, smiling slyly.

"Don't I even get a lawyer?"

"You are a trial, user," the Enchanter said, rolling his eyes. "You should have stayed on your side of the monitor."

"I wish I had," I said and swallowed the lump in my throat.

"Oh, very well, you may have a lawyer," the Enchanter said. He blew a whistle.

Stinky strolled onto the super chip. The computer bug was dressed in a striped suit. The bug carried a jar containing the head of Logic.

Illogic walked behind Stinky. His head was still twisted on his shoulders, so his face tried to run backward. Illogic fumbled and stumbled across the super-chip. He was dressed in a black robe, and his pipe stuck out from a long, white wig that fell in ringlets to his back. He carried a briefcase.

The Enchanter rubbed his hands together and laughed. "I have just downloaded a law degree from the Internet, a plug-in to Illogic's program. Say hello to your lawyer, user. Illogic will defend you for killing his brother with the virus."

"But that's so unfair," Axel yelled.

"What fragment are you from, that you dare to question us, Ghost?" the Enchanter said.

"I am a fragment of her brother's doppelganger."

"Come down here then." The Enchanter pointed his wand at Axel and levitated him to the superchip.

"An eye-for-an-eye is fair, is it not, Brother?" the Enchanter said to Axel. The Enchanter smiled at me. "And you didn't think we had religion here, did you, user?"

"You have a Bible in the archives," I said.

The Enchanter had a gleam in his eyes. "Defend the user," he ordered.

134

Mumblings erupted from Illogic, like the village idiot. He talked to himself, with his head facing east. He responded with his head facing west. He asked questions with his head looking up to the North. He answered his questions looking down to the South. He flung his hands in the air in argument with himself.

"Enough! The trial software has expired," The Enchanter said.

Slowly, the judges vanished.

B. Austin, Belinda Austin

EVER BEEN VOMITED BY A TRASHCAN?

The Enchanter said to the dragon, "Bring in the recycle bin, Draggy." Voila! A trashcan appeared.

The Enchanter pointed the wand at the recycle bin. "Here is the witness for your next trial, Jupiter. Open sesame!"

The lid popped open, revealing Louse-the-Mouse sleeping in the trash.

The Enchanter again pointed the wand. "Wake up, you idiot wheelman!"

Louse's blue tongue hung out, and its dazed eyes opened. "Louse must find his center, center," the mouse said repeatedly. It shook its head and crawled from the bin.

I was not the only one happy that the mouse was salvaged from the trash. Axel moved his mouth to my ear and whispered. "Your brother has the mouse back. Perhaps, Axel can find a way to get you out of here."

"What have you to do with the user Jupiter?" the Enchanter asked Louse.

"I don't remember, Governor," Louse said.

"Then I shall have to remember for you." The Enchanter shot lasers from his eyes, hypnotizing Louse and me.

The Enchanter released us, and we spun in circles.

"The hacker Dormouse gave Jupiter access to our system files," the Enchanter, howled, turning purple.

The Enchanter disappeared in a cloud of smoke.

He materialized, standing on his head. "You make us inefficient, Jupiter! We save the rodent from the recycle bin and because of you, must permanently delete him. Fraggy, purge the mouse."

Grim Reaper picked up the sobbing Louse and carried the mouse over to Fraggy, who resembled a giant green dumpster on legs.

Fraggy opened its huge metal mouth that had jagged, teeth-like edges.

Grim Reaper threw Louse in.

The metal mouth slammed shut.

The audience cringed at the muffled squeaks between the grinding of metal teeth.

The Enchanter floated above me, smiling. "The disk-defragger, Fraggy, will sweep clean the address attached to your brother, so other programs can move into his space. In other words, Axel is not to be recycled."

"Don't worry about me, Jupiter," Axel whispered, "I'm just a ghost. You must not endanger yourself more. You may still have a chance to escape. I overheard that annoying cyber-being talking about a portal."

"I'm sorry, Axel," I said, sobbing.

The Enchanter roared, "Listen carefully to the mouse's suffering. In this same manner, every trace of your brother's existence will be wiped out, as though he never was."

"No!" I dropped to my knees, begging.

Axel hung his ghostly head in defeat. He placed a hand on my shoulder. "Don't feel bad, Jupiter. I'm just a fragment, after all."

The Enchanter lifted his hands to the cyber creatures, who sat captivated by the entertainment. "Hear us all. Our sentence is that the hacker Jupiter be deleted forever." The Enchanter pounded a gavel and turned a thumb down.

The audience cheered.

"You can't exterminate Jupiter. Her technology is mine," a voice cackled with glee. "I intend to turn her into a phone app."

It was the witch, riding a broom and waving her patent documents.

"No scrap of paper commands us! Off with your head!" the Enchanter shouted. He pointed the wand at the witch, zapping her.

The witch fell off her broom. Her head rolled into the swirling pit.

The Enchanter must have memory problems. He forgot about his threat to execute Axel first. "Off with your head," he said, aiming the wand at me.

"Run, Jupiter," Axel yelled.

Grim Reaper grabbed my arms. I kicked out but was too high in the air to strike.

The Gnome King suddenly appeared. He spoke through a bullhorn. "Enchanter, zap me into a desktop icon. I shall stop the virus and spare your life."

"You shall spare our life? Midget!" the Enchanter yelled.

"Do not call me a midget!" The Gnome King stomped like a two-year-old having a temper tantrum. "Make me an icon, or I'll take the virus to the Internet and infect the entire world. Everyone will blame your computer, Enchanter."

The super-chip glowed green, and a yellow light surrounded the Enchanter. "Do not dare to blackmail us," the Enchanter roared.

I BROKE SOME LINKS

The Enchanter turned the Gnome King into a stone garden statue. The Enchanter sniffled as if he had a cold. "We are running low on power due to the virus." He sneezed.

"Quiet!" he yelled at the gasping crowd.

The witch refused to let go of the patent on a digital girl, namely me. Her head was still talking, demanding that the Enchanter release me into her custody.

"Stop your infernal nagging, hag!" The Enchanter yelled.

The witch opened her mouth to speak.

The Enchanter blew a fart, shutting the witch up with magic gas.

"Backup," Axel said in a panicky voice.

"Are you questioning our memory?" the Enchanter growled.

I pointed to the fleas flying over the darkening sky. "Backup," I screeched.

The Enchanter rapped Illogic on his head. "Nitwit, why didn't you remember the *backup* file? We can save ourselves, by restoring to a point in time before the virus struck. Send for the file clerk, Sir Broken-Links."

Everyone danced on their seats, while Illogic ran backwards to fetch the file clerk.

I did cartwheels.

Axel spun on one finger.

Neat! The *backup* file would restore the computer to before the virus struck. Maybe we would go back in time to a period before the gnomes kidnapped me.

A crystal ball rolled across the super-chip. The ball glowed, revealing the image of file cabinets. Drawers slid open and files flipped open. The crystal ball put on reading glasses, scanning papers in the files.

A white mist swirled around the glass ball, lips forming in the mist. "Some files are missing from the *backup* and *recovery* folders, my master."

"What files, Sir Broken-Links?" the Enchanter said, his voice icing.

"The *boot* file," the crystal ball said in a loud, whispery voice.

"But how will we restart? Being without a *boot* file is like trying to start a car without a key," the Enchanter said.

"Other files have vanished. My prediction is that the backup and recovery process is too unstable. If you proceed on this dangerous path, we may be shut down, forever," the ball added in an ominous tone.

A hush filled the arena.

Grim Reaper approached the crystal ball with a hammer held over her head.

The ball glowed red. "Do not shatter me. I am not responsible for this mess! The last time I rolled down the backup tree, all was in order. Someone has broken vital directory branches and thrown files away."

"We shall conduct a séance to discover what happened to the missing files," the Enchanter said.

A table dropped in front of the Enchanter, along with three zombies seated around the table. The zombies were computer forensic tools used to dig up files involving computer crimes.

The Enchanter sat in the fourth chair beside the zombies. A spotlight shone on the Enchanter, and he went into a trance. "We are channeling the spirit of Ada Lovelace, the woman who wrote the first computer program in 1842, for the Babbage Analytical Engine, the first computer. My dear Ada, are you there?"

"I'm here, Enchanter," a sweet voice said in a British accent.

"Show us what happened to the *boot* file. Can you do that, Honey Bunches?"

"Oh, Axel, I did a bad thing in the file room," I whispered.

Axel groaned.

The spotlight shone on my head. Ghostly images played in the background of me in the file room.

The Enchanter thundered, "You are to suffer the fate that was to be Sir Broken-Links. We will shatter you, user. First, you must watch your brother die."

Suddenly, the stinging fleas attacked with a vengeance.

The virus weakened the Enchanter. His servers helped him to rise. "We have such a headache. Our memory leaks," the Enchanter moaned, stumbling on his robe.

Everyone screamed and ran for their lives from the *Arena of Memory Chips*.

I stumbled behind Axel.

Fraggy, the disk-defragger, chased us with its stomach open like a garbage dumpster.

The dumpster clawed at my leg.

I shook my foot, trying to dislodge its claw.

Fraggy twisted and spun, inching its jaws closer.

Suddenly, I was snatched by the neck and sucked up like a vacuum.

Something carried me upward.

Fraggy snapped its jaws at me.

Chills crawled up my spine at the steaming computer, filled with fog and smoke.

There was a jolt, followed by an eerie stillness.

Eek! The virus deleted me! I could not see my hand in front of my face.

There was another jerk.

Whoosh!

I rode on a lightning-fast ride and screamed my head off. It felt as if I was whirling through a tunnel at the speed of light. I kept rubbing my body and patting my head to make sure the virus was not deleting me.

I'm headed to the internet and duplication. I'm going mobile. I'll shrink even smaller. There will be thousands of me or more on cell phones. I'll never get back home now!

OH, HEAVENS!!

Flash! I was back in the study, hanging onto a USB thumb drive. I was never so happy to see my awesome brother.

Axel grinned down at me. "Using the ghostly fragment of my doppelganger, I was able to pull you back with my *personal data transport*," my brother said.

Oddly, I do not remember the USB Flash Drive being an inch bigger than my arm. The USB drive was called a thumb drive because it was the size of a thumb. Yes, I was back but...I was the size of the 11-inch monitor screen.

"It's not funny!" I yelled at Axel.

My giant brother picked me up by the armpits as he would a doll. "Geez, you're flat, Jupiter. No wonder you could hitch a ride on the flash-drive," he said, chuckling. "But I wonder you're no longer smaller than the thumb drive. Somehow you grew a bit."

I tried to punch and kick him.

Axel swung me around, making me dizzy.

"Let me go, creep!" I shouted.

"That's the thanks I get for saving you, little sister? Geez, you look funny. Our kitten is bigger than you are."

I kicked him.

"Your shoe tickles," he said, laughing.

"Let me down," I screeched. I grabbed onto his nostril and bit down hard.

"Ouch! That stings. Okay, there." Axel set me gently down on the rug and then kneeled so he would not have to stoop to my shortness.

"How am I supposed to grow even bigger? Look at me! I'm like 14 inches tall," I said.

"Quit laughing," I yelled.

"I'm not laughing," Axel said.

"Shut up! Quit giggling," I hollered.

"I'm not giggling. You shut up!" Axel said.

"I told you to stop chuckling."

"I'm not chuckling!"

The laughter may have been coming from behind me. I was so little it was hard to tell. The vomit-green carpet was like ankle-deep grass. "Figure out how to maximize my size!"

"Only if you stop acting mean."

"You owe me, Jupiter, and not just for sending a USB Flash Drive to get you out. I covered for you. Between trying to help you and telling Mom I gave you permission to spend the night at your friend's house, I got in trouble. Mom hit the roof, ordering me to clear it next time with her or Dad."

"We need to get our stories straight. What friend did I stay with?"

"Sally, that phreak, the only real friend you have."

"Sally gave up phreaking, because her mom gave her a cell phone with free long-distance service, so she doesn't have to hack into phone systems anymore. Instead, Sally hacks into computers now. I swear my days of hacking are over after this crazy adventure."

Communication with the shadowy, ghostly Axel had been so much easier. "Well, thanks for all your help," I mumbled, regretting every mean trick I ever played on Axel.

The door was still on the study floor. Dickens, our black and white kitty, ran into the room.

His fur stood on end. Dickens crouched low and hissed.

I screamed, and grew a bit.

Dickens reached out its claws, and I shrieked, growing bigger.

The cat opened its mouth and I wailed, growing another inch.

"That's it, Jupiter! Breathe deeply. I forgot that oxygen regulates human cell growth. The fresh air when you exited the computer probably made you grow the size of the monitor screen," Axel said. He grabbed a science book from the bookcase and started fluttering the pages.

I bawled and hollered, taking in gobs of oxygen, to fuel my temper. I wanted to box Axel's ears. It was just like my brother, to be more interested in science than the fact that Dickens was trying to put me in his mouth. Our cat's teeth kept sliding off my paper-thin body.

Yuck! Dickens slobbered spoiled-tuna saliva all over me. I smelled like dead fish.

At last, I grew to my normal height and growled at the cat.

Dickens ran from the room with his tail between his legs.

I was exhausted with growing pains. Cat slobber stuck to my hair. So many things were broken in the study. The mirror was...

"Eek! I am normal-sized but a flat freak! I can't go to school, ever again!"

"Breathe, Jupiter, breathe," Axel said.

I sucked in my breath.

I sucked out my breath.

I ended up over breathing. I hyperventilated which felt as if I could not breathe. I was breathing too fast and felt dizzy. My eyes spun in circles, the study twirling.

Poof! I inflated, mushroomed, and fattened. "Eek! I'm going to blow up like a balloon!" I lay on the carpet, like a fat beetle on its back unable to even roll over.

"Jupiter, calm down. Push all the oxygen from your lungs, until your stomach touches your spine."

"That's it. Suck in your gut, as long as possible. Keep your mouth closed; expand your stomach, slowly."

I did as Axel instructed and sucked my stomach into the rug.

As I grew thinner, the study vibrated with screeches, sounding like a balloon deflating.

At last, I was back to my normal three-dimensional size.

Bam! Bam!

There were two crashes in the room.

B. Austin, Belinda Austin

I'M GROUNDED FOR
THE REST OF MY LIFE

Dad hurried into the room, nearly tripping on the door that was on the floor. For no reason, the lamp fell from the bookcase about the same time Dad came into the room.

Dad stepped over me. He pointed at Axel, who was sitting at the desk with his hand on the game controller. "How many times must I tell you, Axel, that it's just a video game? You get so upset, if you lose. I just fixed that computer and you broke it. Moreover, you cracked the new monitor. When did you break the window? And what happened to the door?" Dad yelled, scowling at my brother.

"I broke the computer," I blurted out. "I'm to blame, Dad, for all the damage."

Dad stood over me with his fists on his hips. "You are going to pay for the broken lamp from your allowance, young lady."

I noticed a quick movement on the bookcase, followed by loud giggling.

Dad shook his finger in my face and shouted, "This is not funny, young lady."

I had not laughed. I knew who shoved the lamp off the bookcase, and it was neither Axel nor me.

The top shelf of the bookcase belonged to Axel. Books about sailing, dog breeds, and science fiction novels filled his shelf.

The bottom bookshelf was mine. This shelf contained novels about witches, humorous cat stories, and classic books.

We shared the middle shelf. Computer pirating magazines leaned against computer hacking magazines. At Axel's shelf end was a figure of an eye-patched pirate. At my end was a pony-tailed girl, waving a sword, hacking at a ceramic computer.

Something had grabbed onto my ankle right before I hitched a ride on the USB flash drive. March-Hare, my doppelganger the other Jupiter, and a gnome had hidden in the Personal Data Transporter and escaped the computer through the USB port with me. However, they were all still small.

March-Hare was the size of a bookend and pushed against the magazines. She was always a 3-D avatar so the spectacled bunny did not look odd. March-Hare now pretended to be a white statue of a rabbit wearing a yellow polka dot bow. Aha! March-Hare blinked behind her computer glasses.

The gnome and the other Jupiter were flat, just as I had been. My doppelganger was about a foot tall. The redheaded gnome was only about seven inches tall. They both stood on the same shelf as March-Hare. The other Jupiter was at the right end, flat up against the wood, appearing like wallpaper on the bookcase shelf. The gnome did the same on the other end of the shelf.

Neither Dad nor Axel noticed anything odd about the bookcase.

March-Hare, the gnome, and my doppelganger all giggled again in unison, so it sounded like one loud laugh.

"You're still laughing?" Dad said to me.

"Yes," I quickly said, shifting my eyes to the snickering figures on the bookcase, and then back to my father.

Dad leaned closer. "Read my lips. You're grounded, Jupiter."

I opened my mouth and laughed very loud in order to mask the laughter coming from the bookcase.

"What in tarnation happened to your braces?" Dad asked.

"I sort of lost my braces."

"For the rest of your life, you are grounded. Do you hear me, young lady?"

I nodded my head yes, of course, whatever you say, Dad. Sir. Sir Dad.

"Now clean up as much of this mess as you can," Dad said.

He patted Axel on the back. The two left the study, gossiping about me.

"You sister is a brat," Dad said.

"Ah, Jupiter is not so bad, Dad," Axel said.

"But how can anyone lose their braces? How is that even possible?"

"With Jupiter, anything is possible. My sister is a pro," Axel proudly said.

Their voices faded.

The three came out of hiding.

The gnome and my miniature doppelganger were no longer flat due to the oxygen from laughing. However, they were small.

Quick, I tried to grab my doppelganger, but the other Jupiter scurried from the study. Like most hackers, I was not athletic except for my typing fingers. Cyber creatures were slippery little suckers. I spun and all three had vanished from the room.

Pictures dropped from the hall walls, crashing to the floor.

The hallway became littered with broken glass, which made it hard for me to chase them since I was barefoot.

The other Jupiter spun and grinned at me. She held the gnome's hand. The gnome was a bearded, ordinary-looking gnome. The gnome had already been in my bedroom and was dressed in fashion-doll clothes. I now regretted not throwing my last doll out. The gnome looked ridiculous, dressed in a loose, red, sequined dress. His cone hat tilted jauntily on his head, and his beard came to a point at his waist. He looked even sillier wobbling on yellow, plastic, high-heel sandals. The heels were tight, the straps bending his flat feet.

The gnome snarled at me and glared with beady eyes.

March-Hare hopped in front of them.

The bunny stopped hopping to take a poop on the hall rug.

My parents would blame Dickens for those pellets.

March-Hare then punched a hole in the wall and hopped sideways. She was still a crazy bunny.

I was about to run after the rascals when Dad yelled from downstairs, "Jupiter, what did you break now?"

The three strolled down the hallway and into my parents' bedroom. Gnomes loved clothes. The beastie was probably going through Mom's dresser. Gnomes were good with a needle and thread. The gnome was probably making an outfit from mom's underwear.

Even more socks were going to vanish because gnomes were known for stealing from clothes dryers, which was the secret to vanishing socks.

In the future, my family would blame me for any mischief done by my doppelganger, March Hare, and the gnome.

"Jupiter, I'm not going to tell you again to come down and eat your supper," Dad yelled.

"We're waiting for you," Mom shouted.

I did not even have time to clean up. I shuffled on dirty feet, towards the stairs.

With those three creatures causing trouble in my house, I really was grounded for the rest of my life. Bummer!

I had to admit though that it was a wondrous adventure!

Mm, being distributed on apps might have been mind-blowing.

Oh, well, I was glad to be home.

"I'm coming!" I hollered.

I slid down the bannister and laughed. My parents hated when I took shortcuts.

AWESOME READER

Thank you so much for reading *Digital Girl*. I hope you enjoyed this Action–Adventure of Fantasy, Science Fiction, and Technology, that may have been written by computer gnomes.

If you enjoyed my creation, please consider **Reviewing Digital Girl** so that others may discover it. Because the writing field is so competitive, reviews help me purchase advertising so that I can spread the word about my books.

If you do not wish to leave a review then, "No worries."

All my best,

B. Austin

DIGITAL GIRL